DAWN OF VICTORY

Also by Louis Fischer
MEN AND POLITICS

DAWN OF VICTORY

LOUIS FISCHER

DUELL, SLOAN AND PEARCE
NEW YORK

COPYRIGHT, 1942, BY
LOUIS FISCHER

All rights reserved, including the right to reproduce this book or portions thereof in any form.

first edition

PRINTED IN THE UNITED STATES OF AMERICA

Everywhere breaks the dawn and the light spreads, blood-red but clear.

—WINSTON CHURCHILL, Ottawa,
December 30, 1941.

CONTENTS

INTRODUCTION	ix
1. NEW YORK TO LONDON	3
2. THE BRITISH PEOPLE	21
3. FIGHTER PILOTS	49
4. LONDON SPEAKING	69
5. CHURCHILL AND THE BRITISH GOVERNMENT	81
6. WHITHER ENGLAND?	111
7. WHAT WILL RUSSIA DO?	139
8. AMERICA'S NEW ROLE IN WORLD AFFAIRS	173
9. THE STRATEGY OF VICTORY	189
10. THE SHAPE OF THE PEACE TO COME	223
INDEX	263

INTRODUCTION

THE United States is at war. Americans should not underestimate the enemies arrayed against them. Americans should know the strength and weakness of their friends. Exact knowledge is a prerequisite of victory.

LOUIS FISCHER

NEW YORK TO LONDON

1. NEW YORK TO LONDON

I HAD to go to England.

I saw England at war in 1918. I saw it often between the two wars. I saw it just after the second world war began. I wanted to see it again after its two years of combat with Hitler Germany.

I wanted to know what were the elements of strength, and of weakness, in the British position. What can Britain contribute to victory? How long can England hold out? Would it make peace if Hitler offered peace? What was the secret of Churchill's power and influence? What were England's old politicians doing? Were new men coming to the fore? Suppose Churchill dies?

British women, I knew, had played a vital role in Britain's defense. What had happened to their nerves, their spirit, and their interests? What had enabled the people to "take it"?

Is Germany's strength waning? What about the slave peoples in Nazi-dominated Europe?

How much can England do for Russia? What can Russia do for England and China? What changes have taken place in Russia since the ugly period of Soviet-Nazi collaboration? How does the Russo-German war affect the strategy of victory?

What are the British thinking? Are they satisfied

with their government's conduct of the war? What about Labor? Is England going socialist? Are the distinctions between rich and poor being wiped out?

How would the British treat a defeated Germany? What peace would be made this time? Will the world be better and safer to live in after the war?

I learned more in England than I had expected to learn. I learned about British plans and prospects. I understand British psychology better. I admire the British more. I talked at length to most of the members of the British government, to scores of members of Parliament, to trade-union leaders, to big business men, to little business men, to bus drivers, RAF pilots, to women, to children, to miners at pitheads, to workingmen in steel mills, to soldiers, writers, artists, and government officials. I saw much, heard much, felt much, and kept a detailed diary of the experience. It was a rich and exciting experience.

I went to Europe by Clipper. These giant seaplanes cross the ocean several times a week and we read about them in the newspapers. But it is still a startling achievement. Eight thousand feet above the endless sea you leave your soft comfortable seat, walk over to a big table where food is waiting—meat, salad, bread and butter, coffee, ice water, ice cream. You fill your plate and cup. You return to your seat and consume your food in company with fellow passengers. Then you loll back and smoke or read, or sleep. I used to take walks up and down the corridor, which is as long as a Pullman car and much smoother to promenade in.

Breakfast and lunch are prepared on board and served at tables set up in the various sections of the Clipper. Two stewards act as waiters. In the evening they make up the berths which are bigger than those on a train.

The Clipper, a huge flying boat, is run with quiet, unostentatious efficiency by ten young men. Between watches they sometimes come downstairs into the body of the Clipper to answer the silly questions of the passengers. Normally, a Clipper consumes two hundred gallons of gasoline an hour. The flight from New York to Bermuda took us five hours, from Bermuda to Horta, an island in the Portuguese Azores, fourteen hours, and from there to Lisbon seven hours. For the Bermuda-Horta stretch the Clipper carries three thousand gallons of gasoline in addition, of course, to about a ton of mail and anywhere between twenty-five and thirty-five passengers.

Before landing at Bermuda—these Clippers always "land" on the water—all the blinds in the plane were drawn so we could not see the work that has been going on ever since the United States undertook to build a naval base on this British isle. After strict but gentlemanly examination of baggage and of every scrap of printed and written matter, and while I was watching the huge American Catalina seaplanes warm up for Atlantic patrol duty, a British voice announced over the microphone that because of swells at Horta we would remain in Bermuda for twenty-four hours. I asked Captain Winston what a swell was and how he knew that the swell in Horta today would be there tomorrow. He replied that there was no swell at Horta today but there would be one tomorrow and he therefore could not risk bringing down the million-dollar machine tomorrow morning in the Horta harbor. A swell created dangerously high waves.

"But if there is no swell today how do you know there will be one tomorrow?" I asked.

"The swells at Horta are born in Greenland," the captain explained. "When a low-pressure area develops in Greenland it draws to it the air from western Africa and that stirs up the waters around the Azores."

Wonders never cease. The human brain that is able to figure this out cannot devise a way of keeping the world at peace.

For twenty-four hours we stayed in Bermuda—at the Pan American company's expense—until the Horta swells became flatter. The night was tropical and smelled of palms and of the dry grass of the golf course. The next morning I bathed in the quiet translucent waters of the bay and then swam in the hot open-air pool of the Belmont Manor.

There were many young United States sailors about, and an American destroyer, painted somber black, rode in the bay across from the hotel. Apparently, however, Anglo-American union meets with obstacles when it comes to be translated from paper into practice. The Bermuda *Mid-Ocean Times*, daily organ of the leading colonial families, complains that Washington is not "fair" in dealing with the owners of the land which America needs for the new naval base. One "former owner of a very valuable property," the paper writes, "received a letter from the Colonial Secretary asking him to meet an American representative . . . to discuss the value of the land in question." The Britisher came, but "the American representative failed to keep the appointment." The Britisher, accordingly, told the colonial authorities what he considered a fair price for the land. "Nothing more was heard until the owner received notice weeks later that the Arbitrators were desirous of looking at his property. In the meantime, rushed for time, the Americans had felled most of the trees of the property, removed the top soil, covered the entire water front with sand pumped from the harbor and had converted the houses there into barracks. . . . Two weeks later the owner of the property was called before the Arbitrators and given an amount of a little more than half he had asked for." No appeal was permitted. Now comes the startling part of this Bermuda newspaper's contribution to Anglo-American solidarity. "The Americans," it says, "want certain properties in Bermuda, primarily to defend their eastern seaboard. It is their and not our defense which is the primary consideration. That being the case, certainly they should be willing to compensate. . . . This we consider is a moral obligation and if the American government fails to accept it as such then it falls to the Bermuda government as a duty to see that property compensation is commensurate to property replacement." Voila! Defeat Hitler. Aid Britain. But property is property and profits are profits.

The flight from Bermuda to Horta was smooth and pleasant. In the morning I strolled up and down the Clipper corridor. Below were the islands of the Azores, looking like rocks dropped haphazard by a god into the sea. We began to descend. On both sides were mountains, their heads cut off by clouds. We dived down between them, settled on the water with a few slight bumps, and taxied into the breakwater area. The swell was still about three feet high and it required skill to land the Clipper safely on the heaving waves. The S.S. *Isle de Re* was anchored in the little harbor. It had left New York with food for Unoccupied France, gift of the American Red Cross, and was to make regular trips. But this service soon ended when it became clear that anything that helped any part of France, Vichyated or not, helped Hitler. A second freighter swayed just inside the breakwater. Its name was German and as we docked it hoisted the bright red and black swastika flag. That may have given satisfaction to the Nazi seamen who hung over its railings. But their delight is diluted by the knowledge that they are staying at Horta for the duration of the war. A sister German freighter made a dash out of Horta and was immediately picked up outside Portuguese territorial waters and sunk.

Small men and women in black stand about as we land; it is a very poverty-stricken place. The cars of Pan American Airways are hoary and they advance up the hill by taking a few gallops, then a jolt and some more gallops. Finally they pull up the incline to the big house of the Western Union—the transatlantic cable passes near Horta—now shared by Pan American. Here the Fulmars, an attractive young American couple with a little baby boy, live in isolation with a few more Americans who take care of Western Union and Pan

NEW YORK TO LONDON 9

American affairs. The hall of the house is huge and contains an expensive short-wave radio, a ping-pong table and many comfortable chairs. I played ping pong with a fellow passenger, later watched Captain Winston beat Mrs. Fulmar at chess, and then played against him myself. The rain descended in sheets. Someone turned on the radio.

"Altitude 5,000 feet. What is your visibility?" a voice said.

Captain Winston stopped playing. "That's the Clipper coming in from Lisbon," he said.

"Visibility here 1,000 feet," the Pan American man on land replied to the pilot of the Clipper in the air.

"I am landing on estimates," the pilot was heard to say.

"He's landing blind, flying blind," Winston explained.

"Down at 3,000 feet," the Clipper pilot announced a moment later.

"Watch out for high swells just outside the breakwater," the Pan American manager warned him. "Thick rain down here."

"Gee whiz," Winston said, and nervously lit a cigarette.

Nothing for a few seconds. The suspense made one's heart thump. Winston was disturbed because we could not yet hear the motors of the Clipper.

"Where are you?" we heard the manager ask on the radio.

"Down to 1,000 feet. Approaching breakwater," the

Clipper replied. "I can see nothing. Are there any ships inside the harbor?"

"Watch out for the *Isle de Re* in the center of the harbor. Land west of the *Isle de Re*."

"We can see you now," the pilot said.

"That's good," Winston commented and his face relaxed. "But it's going to be a mighty difficult landing."

"Mind the swells," the manager warned again.

"Landing in a minute," the plane said.

Winston fidgeted and flicked the ashes from his cigarette.

"Landed," the Clipper reported. "Taxiing in slowly."

"Phew," Winston whistled with relief, and returned to the chessboard.

"Docked," reported the Clipper.

We waited twenty-eight hours at Horta for the weather to subside and then took off for the last peaceful lap to Lisbon. We landed on the broad Tagus River with the crowded picturesque hill city on our left. I had seen the Tagus when it flowed with blood—in September, 1936—up at Toledo, Spain, where it curls around the walls of the famous Alcazar fortress.

The waters of the Tagus were so rough it took the Clipper an hour to dock. Finally, we alighted and walked down the boards of a long jetty to the customs shed. Portuguese in black stood against a fence near the dock; they smiled. Their faces, I thought, said, "Queer people, to be coming to Europe when all of Europe wants to go to America."

On the map, Spain and Portugal look like Europe's gangplank. The gangplank is crowded with people whom fascism is squeezing out of Europe but who have not yet been able to obtain a ship and a visa for the free world across the ocean. For them, every day is a gamble: odd or even, red or black, Hitler or a visa, seventeen or eighteen on the roulette wheel, the Nazis or a berth on a vessel? Hundreds of them play their luck every night in the casino at Estoril, an hour outside Lisbon.

This casino is the last international. Where else does a German with a saber gash on his cheek sit elbow to elbow with an Englishman? When the S.S. *West Point* disgorged the German and Italian consuls from America into Portugal, high Nazi officials, led by Hans Dieckhoff, ex-ambassador at Washington, met them at the gangplank, and the next evening they flipped chips at Estoril. A Nazi official, with the typical cropped Prussian head, bent over to place his bet on No. 33; as he straightened up, his coat brushed the shoulder of a dark woman who sat next to him. Her eyes were deep and brown, and she bit her fingernails. "Pardon," the Nazi exclaimed, "pardon, Mademoiselle," and bowed sharply from the waist. The girl was Jewish, from Warsaw. He had sent many like her to the concentration camp.

The Nazis had brought their women folk. One *Hausfrau* in diplomatic chic won frequently, and each time she put the big chip winnings into her purse and played with the little ones. Then she said to her husband, "Now I've had enough. Let's go and cash in." In leaving they passed a group of Nazis whom America had declared *personae non gratae*. "Heil Hitler," they said.

"Heil Hitler," came the reply, and stiff Nazi salutes were exchanged.

Ex-Ambassador Dieckhoff stood against a wall and chatted with colleagues. When he smiled in his best effeminate way, his cheeks filled out and became like flasks. I looked at these Nazis, the men and the gawky women, and thought to myself, "Are these the breeders of the 'master race'?" The cold eyes of the men seemed to say, "Next victim!"; the women were ugly and subservient.

Suddenly there was a shrill shriek followed by a thud. The Warsaw girl had fainted and fallen to the floor. The Nazis quit the table. After the girl revived, she felt weak and embarrassed. I invited her to the bar for a drink.

When the Nazis had attacked Poland, she was in Paris studying art. Her father, mother, and four brothers were then in Warsaw. She had not heard from them since. After the fall of France she fled to Spain and later to Portugal. An uncle in Cleveland had sent her some money, and a Latin American consul with whom she went out several times promised her a visa to his country for $100. The day before she had brought him the money, but he had said he did not want her money and did not want her to go away. He wanted her to stay in Portugal with him until he was ready to return home on vacation. So she had gambled last night on her $100 and won $72. This evening she had lost the $172. She cried as she told the story. But then her face grew stern, and she said: "I will fight it through. Two artist friends of mine have committed suicide in the last eight weeks. I will see it through. But I will not gamble any more."

The Japanese appear to be the most nervous gamblers and the White Russians the most serious. The anti-Nazi Germans whisper; the Nazi Germans are the loudest talkers. There were some American pilots and officials, too, just off the Clipper, at this gangplank international. They played more light-heartedly than the others, chucking in a few dollars for the sensation and then going home to bed.

I had a "go" at the roulette wheel. I discovered that when I played the moderate stakes I could afford I got no kick out of it, and when I risked higher sums I got plenty of excitement but lost more than was healthy for my pocketbook. So after a fling I assumed the role of impartial observer, and studied faces, especially eyes, and fingers. The winner is not the person who guesses the right number; he is the one who knows when to go home. I noticed how often people rose to leave, counted their chips, then wandered around looking things over, and hesitantly, took a seat at another table. Many of them have lost home, country, family, career, wealth, friends, all connections, and a lot of hope. They stand, precariously, between Hitler and the deep black sea. Perhaps the flip of a card or a turn of the wheel will bring fortune. More often it does the opposite.

A Belgian countess, fleeing before the Nazi blitz, motored through France and Spain to Lisbon. That was in June, 1940. The same month a French industrialist, summering at Biarritz, avoided capture by the Germans by sailing his yacht around Cape Finisterre to Lisbon.

Here they met a Japanese diplomat whose pro-British attitude had cost him his job. One day a Scottish sea captain was fished out of the water off Portugal after his ship had gone down with a Nazi submarine's torpedo in it. The four were now having a quiet game of bridge at Estoril. The captain, smoking a pipe, explained that they all planned to cross the ocean soon in the Frenchman's yacht and make their homes in Trinidad.

One evening I met George Weller, who was booked to leave the next morning by ship for the mouth of the Congo and thence to cross Africa for his paper, the Chicago *Daily News*. A British journalist was heading for Cairo. He would then go to Palestine, Syria, and Turkey in the hope of making his way to Moscow to cover the Russo-German war. Nazi agents were in Lisbon trying to buy diamonds for Germany's war industries. Italians shuttled between Portugal and Brazil and Peru, where Mussolini's influence is strongest. British secret-service men watched their comings and goings. A Spanish priest, about to depart on a mission to Latin America, confided to friends that General Franco was packing the largest possible number of Falangist hotheads into the Spanish Legion to fight against the Soviet Army. The more of these he got rid of, the easier it would be for the old-style conservatives and landlords and army generals to rule Spain. "There has been hunger," the priest admitted, "but we always have had hunger in Spain." I asked him about Germans in Spain. He replied, "We are the only peaceful vacation land in Europe. German officers, tired from the war, come to us as tourists." He did not laugh.

Spaniards weep. Spain is the unhappiest country on an unhappy continent.

After two visits to the casino, I found Estoril boring and I was glad to get notice from British Imperial Airways that I could have a seat in a plane for somewhere in England.

I left orders to be awakened at five-fifteen. In the morning the telephone bell rang. I put on the light and looked at my watch. It was five. Jay Allen was calling me from Lisbon. He had just arrived from France where he had been imprisoned by the Nazis for several months. We had a long talk. He said German officers he had met were pessimistic about the final outcome of the war.

Our giant landplane left from Cintra, up in the lovely hills above Lisbon. When we got to the airport I saw a great swastika. It was painted on the side of the massive Folke Wulfe passenger plane of the type usually used for bombing operations at sea. The Germans employ this field for their flights from Portugal to Germany. Behind the German machine stood an Italian Savoia, and behind it a Portuguese passenger plane. In front of the Folke Wulfe were the two British machines making the flight that day, one for passengers and freight, the other for mail. Our Douglas warmed up and, to get into position to take on passengers, made a circle which brought its wing right under the nose of the Nazi plane.

Inside our Douglas were two canvas bags containing rubber boats which could be inflated in the water—in case we were shot down. We flew parallel with the

French coast and a Nazi fighter might have taken a leisurely crack at us. We were not armed. Six hours flying with this charming thought! Meanwhile, however, we enjoyed a nice lunch in the air. During the last half-hour, all windows were barred with wooden shutters so that we could see nothing of British coastal defenses or of military preparations inland. It was a relief to jump out on to the terra firma at the aerodrome.

England at war. My first impression was war planes; huge nets over buildings for camouflage effect; men in uniform; hangars painted to conceal them from enemy aircraft.

"Did you have a smooth flight?" asked the corporal with a smile.

"Have a chair," said the sergeant, pushing one towards me.

"Would you come for a spot of tea?" the officer urged.

It was almost as if I had arrived at a country estate for a week-end. Everybody was relaxed, courteous, and smiling. The aerodrome officials had done their duty when they passed us quickly through the immigration and customs inspection. But there was a train soon to London, and they helped carry our luggage into the bus and speeded our way, told us how to buy the rail tickets, and asked solicitously if we had enough English money.

War everywhere. Little homes slit open by bombs so that you can see the furniture and the mirror above the mantelpiece. "V" for victory on the walls left standing.

"Vee Vill Vin" on one ruined cottage. A huge warehouse near the station smashed by the Nazis. The station itself was hit. But trains never stopped running.

The scene at the railway station immediately took me back to 1918 when I first visited England. Once again the station platform, the waiting rooms and the trains were tightly packed with officers and private soldiers. Uniforms everywhere. This time, women in uniforms, uniforms similar in design and color to those of the men; the only difference was that the men wore trousers and the women short skirts.

The soldiers sat around on their kit bags or leaned on their rifles waiting for the train. The officers in suits of better quality and fit carried little attaché cases or suitcases. Many of the officers wore ribbons on their chests for the medals they had won in the first world war. In one corner I noticed two men, obviously father and son. The father, about forty-five, an army major, slightly gray around the temples, was a veteran of 1914-1918. The son, about twenty-two, was dressed in the blue of the air force. I saw nothing sadder during my entire stay in Britain. Father and son did not look sad; father, when I listened, was recounting some experiences in France in 1917. But it was sad to think that the generation which fought the "war to end wars," and then fathered sons and daughters to live in peace, was now fighting a second world war in company with those sons and daughters. Just as the new generation reached maturity it stepped into battle.

In the train I felt as though I were watching a tennis game: every ten seconds I looked to one side and then through the opposite window to the other side. Aeroplanes in the air, camps on the ground, anti-aircraft balloons swaying in the wind, cattle grazing, factories smoking, farm equipment left out in the field to interfere with the landing of Nazi aeroplanes bringing invasion troops, soldiers and girls holding hands on quaint country roads, wayside stations jammed with troops, women porters in blue trousers, freight trains laden with new guns and tanks, more aeroplanes cavorting in the sky. And then London.

The taxi drove through streets I knew. Every street showed the marks of bombs. Here was war at its most frightful, war on civilians, a war that strikes the kitchens of small homes, that smashes the baby's bed, that kills a family of four at the dinner table.

THE BRITISH PEOPLE

2. THE BRITISH PEOPLE

SHORTLY after I arrived in England I met an old friend, Margaret Storm Jameson, the distinguished novelist. I asked where her father was. Her father is eighty-eight. "In Whitby," she replied. Whitby is on the east coast of England just where the Nazis, after crossing the North Sea, come over British territory to launch their air raids. "But hasn't he been bombed out?" I asked. "Only his windows have been shattered," she replied. I asked why she had not moved her father to a safer place inland. "What!" she exclaimed. "It's his house. He was born in it. Do you think I would leave my house because Hitler might bomb it?"

John Strachey, ex-Communist, author and lecturer, has been a flying officer in the RAF since 1940. I saw him in London three days after my arrival. He asked me what it cost to fly the ocean. I told him and wondered why he wanted to know. "My wife and two children are in Canada," he said, "and I want to bring them back here."

"But aren't they better off where they are?" I suggested. His children are five and eight years old.

"No," he replied. "England is living through its greatest experience in history, and my children will be poorer Englishmen if they do not share the experience."

Strachey is not alone in thinking so.

The British have an instinctive sense of being where they belong. They mean to stay there. The British nation has found itself in war. I was in England several months before the war broke out. The country was jittery and tormented by mental doubts. It was divided and nervous. The war came. The nation settled down to a long, difficult task without wincing and without illusions.

The Chamberlain era was one of national humiliation. Peace, purchased at the price of surrender, increased the danger of war, and it made the nation ashamed of itself. Hitler became a symbol to Britain of its helplessness. That is gone now.

The British were equally irked by the "phony" war period in 1939 and 1940. An Englishwoman was talking to me about those months of inactivity. "It would have been awful," she said, "if things hadn't got worse." Things did get worse, and the people got better. At an evening party in England some persons were saying that cigarettes were worse since the war started, newspapers were worse, transportation was worse, in fact everything was worse.

"Only the people are better," one man interjected.

The people are wonderful.

Winston Churchill said to me in an off-the-record interview, "There will be no flinching here." I believe it. The greatness of Churchill is that he personifies and intensifies the greatness of the British people in the present crisis.

Churchill frequently visits cities that have been bombed by the Germans. While I was in England the newspapers printed a photograph of Churchill in the much-punished city of Plymouth. He was shown walking down the center of a narrow street. In the corner of his mouth was the inevitable cigar. He wore his best grin. In front of him, behind him, on both sides of him walked men, women, and children. He was in the middle of a spontaneous popular demonstration. Almost above his head some folks were cheering him from a first-floor balcony and he had taken off his Homburg hat, put it on his cane, and was waving it high in the air. That was a photograph of democracy. When Mussolini appears to the populace it is from a very elevated second-story balcony and the multitude is kept at least a hundred yards from the building. It is years since either Stalin or Hitler has been seen among unknown, uncounted citizens who just happened to be around. The dictators are surrounded by spies, detectives, and trusted henchmen who build a wall between leader and masses. Dictators fear their people; hence the rigors of dictatorship. Churchill does not fear the British people.

"Why does no one kill Hitler?" the curious ask. The answer is simple: those who wish to kill Hitler can never get near him and those who are near him don't want to kill him.

The British know that if they lose the war they will lose their democratic freedom and their rights as human beings and become the slaves of the Nazi conqueror or of his British Quisling, assuming one could be found. England has the horrible example of a whole continent to warn it against surrender and to spur it on to unending effort for victory. A great Spanish woman once said

—and President Roosevelt later repeated her words—"It is better to die on one's feet than to live on one's knees." The British look across the Channel and see the French living on their knees. The Spanish government is the friend of Hitler; Spain is starving. Italy is the ally of Hitler; Italy has become a German colony. Czechoslovakia was not allowed to resist Hitler; the Czechs are now, under compulsion, manufacturing the weapons which strengthen their oppressor. The Rumanians and Hungarians thought they would save themselves by joining Hitler's camp; they are pouring out their blood to further Hitler's conquest. Stalin hoped to remain at peace by entering into a compact with Hitler and looting their neighbors together; in his own good time Hitler betrayed the Moscow appeasers and laid their land waste. The recorded fate of European countries shows the British that there is no way of living with Hitler. He must be destroyed.

It took the British a long time to make up their minds about Hitler. It always takes the British a long time to make up their minds. But once their minds are made up —try to unmake them. Strange that anybody should want war. The newsreels, radio, photographs, and the tales of foreign correspondents have brought the horrors of war to the eye, ear, and heart of every human. If war was hell in the nineteenth century what would be the correct word in the twentieth? Yet the British people went to war from choice. They decided that "this fellow Hitler" had to be stopped. They would not go on being kicked around by him. Life would never be quiet until he was licked. That is how the British felt in September, 1939, and that is why Great Britain went to war. On September 1, Hitler invaded Poland. The next day the House of Commons met in London in a tense atmosphere. England had officially guaranteed the independence of Poland. Would England, accordingly, go to war? Prime Minister Neville Chamberlain made a vague statement to Parliament. He did not say England would declare war on the Nazis. Arthur Greenwood, acting leader of the Labor Party—Attlee was ill at the time—rose to answer Chamberlain. Just as Greenwood got on his feet, Robert Boothby, a Tory member of Parliament, yelled across the House to Greenwood, "Speak for England." * That was the most remarkable call heard in the British Parliament. A Tory M.P. was implying that his own leader, the Prime Minister, no longer spoke for the country. He was implying that Labor might speak for the country. Greenwood delivered a fighting, vigorous speech. Conservatives, too, were in revolt against Chamberlain's vacillation. They had been in touch with their voters during the summer and they knew that the mood of the people was for resistance to Hitler. The next day was Sunday. At eleven in the morning England declared war. The people had forced the government to go to war. That is how the people's war started.

Hitler and Goebbels have proclaimed their aim: the destruction of the British Empire and the creation of a Nazi New Order. More people see this today than on September 3, 1939. That is why the British determination to go on is as strong as steel. The clearest im-

---

* According to some persons, this exclamation was made by L. S. Amery. Hansard, the official stenographic record of Parliamentary debates, omits the name but gives the exclamation.

pression I brought back from England is that the British will not quit. They will wage war until they win or are decisively defeated.

One of my journalistic assignments in England was to delve into the mystery of the flight of Rudolph Hess to Scotland. Cabinet ministers were willing to discuss almost anything with me off the record. But when I said to them, "And could you give me any hint as to Hess's purpose in coming here?" these men, who had read all the verbatim records of the Nazi deputy's testimony in England, would say, "Sorry, I really know nothing about this matter." Their lips are sealed. A London editor, talking to me about the secrecy surrounding the Hess affair, said, "Never has so much been withheld from so many by so few." The reason is that Hess is Churchill's own prisoner, and Churchill has enjoined silence on his colleagues.

I received many refusals for information on Hess, but when I compared the refusals I learned something. Moreover, lesser men talk where top leaders do not. What I set down here is not my thesis or theory about the Hess flight. Nor is it an interpretation of facts. It is merely facts as I collected them in official circles:

When Hess dropped from heaven by parachute and was captured by a Scot with a pitchfork he said he would talk to no one but Churchill or Foreign Secretary Anthony Eden. The British intermediary told him that no British leader would talk to a Nazi. The British intermediary was Ivone Kirkpatrick with whom I talked several times in the British Foreign Office. He was formerly an official in the British Embassy in Berlin, and there he met Hess, but Hess did not remember him. That was unpleasant; yet no matter.

For two weeks Hess persisted vainly in demanding a confrontation with Churchill or Eden. In the third week he broke down and talked. He said Germany was about to attack Russia. That was three weeks before Hitler's invasion of Russia. Churchill forthwith sent a telegram to Stalin warning him of the impending assault.

In view of the imminent Russo-German war, Hess said, England ought to call off the war against Germany. If Britain stopped fighting Germany or actually helped Germany, Russia could be smashed in three months, Hess stated. If Germany had to cope with Russia and England, the conquest of Russia would, in his opinion, last a year.

Kirkpatrick explained that the war was the will of the people and that Churchill, even if he wished, could not end the war by negotiation. "You're not serious?" Hess exclaimed. The totalitarian mind is incapable of understanding the democratic process.

To Hess's proposal of a separate peace the British returned a simple answer in one word: "No." Hess was shocked. In that case, he said, he wanted an aeroplane, gasoline, and maps to fly back to Germany. He received his second shock when the answer was again a simple "No."

Hitler made peace with Stalin in August, 1939, and remained at peace with Russia until he had knocked out France, the Low Countries, Scandinavia, and the Balkans. Then he turned on Russia. While he was knocking out Russia he wanted peace with England. Then he could turn on England. England said: No. The British, at last, had grasped this Nazi technique of "one by one."

During my nine weeks in England, I conducted my own Gallup poll. To every person with whom I had a conversation of any length—probably two hundred people—I said, "Suppose Hitler makes you a peace offer. What will you do?" Only one person replied that peace would be worth considering. All others rejected the idea with varying degrees of vehemence and profanity.

I had been talking to the managing director of a big steel mill in Yorkshire. We discussed efficiency of production, labor conditions, government interference with operations, and so forth. He was urbane, a gentleman. Then I posed my question about a negotiated peace. He grew red; he breathed heavily. He obviously imposed restraint on himself, but shouted, nevertheless, "What, with that blackguard? With that bloody scoundrel? Never."

"All right," I said. "Suppose you rebuff him. He bombs you and you bomb him for a year and then he makes another peace offer?"

Words were no good any more. The managing director bit his lips and shook his head quickly to the right and left. No, no, no. I got the same response from workingmen, soldiers, officials, Cabinet ministers, and women air-raid wardens.

There is no way back; they must go on and take it. It is not easy to take it. Signs in many London streets read: "To the Trenches." They startle one into a realization that all England is a Flanders crisscrossed by trenches. And this time the trenches are filled not with soldiers but with women, civilian men, and with children. Civilians have been fighting this war as much as soldiers, in fact, more than the British Army in Britain. They tell the story of a private in the army who received a letter from his grandmother saying that she had just extinguished six incendiary bombs.

In the air-raid blitzes, the British showed their best face. Several Frenchmen and Spaniards who lived through that period in England assured me they would never return to their native countries; they had fallen in love with the British. The British behaved with a casual nonchalance and valor that inspired admiration. But when I said to my British publisher, "Your people have been wonderful," he replied airily, "Oh, no. What is one to do? You can either yell and go crazy or commit suicide when the bombs fall. Or you can behave and be quiet." (Ten million new books belonging to publishing houses, he told me, were destroyed in the blitzes.)

The British were hard, tough, and philosophical. The British learned to be proud of one another. They showed strength and dignity. They were the gallant knights one had dreamed of in one's youth. Juan del Vayo, the son of the Loyalist Foreign Minister, told me in London that he was eating a meal in a restaurant with another Spaniard when bombs began to drop near-by. Both ducked under a table. When they came up, an Englishman at a neighboring table said to them, "And why did you do that?"

"We thought it would be safer," Vayo replied.

"But what about your dignity?" the Englishman exclaimed.

Most of the time I was in London I lived in a big villa, on the edge of the royal parks of London, as guest of George Russell Strauss, a Labor member of Parliament. Fellow guests were Aneurin Bevan, another Labor M.P., and Mrs. Bevan who is Jennie Lee, a former M.P. Once I stepped out of the house into the driveway and saw five little girls. The oldest had been carrying the youngest piggy-back, and they were all obviously tired and had come in to rest. The two smallest were crying and all seemed sad. I said, "Do you like chocolate?" Their eyes opened, and when I returned with some candy from my room their tears had dried and their faces were joyous again. They were workingmen's children from two families, the oldest eleven, the youngest two and a half. They had not left London since the war started.

"Do the bombs frighten you?" I asked.

"No," they replied cheerfully.

"We like the blitz," the oldest said. "It's exciting."

"What do you do?" I inquired. "Do you go down into the shelters?"

"No," the oldest explained. "We stay under the beds and keep shouting, 'Mummy, can we come out?' "

During the heavy air raids of October, 1940, only 470,000 Londoners used the public shelters in subways or specially constructed subterranean chambers. Just over two million people resorted to private shelters, usually the Anderson shelter, named after Sir John Anderson, member of the War Cabinet. The Anderson consists of a semi-circular sheet of corrugated iron and a front and back wall of the same material. The structure is embedded in the earth of a garden or yard and covered with earth, and only a front door is left open for entrance and escape. These Andersons proved satisfactory. But at least half of London stayed in their homes, often in reinforced basements, sometimes in their apartments. Apartment houses built on steel girders stood up best under Hitler's blows. The old slum houses, two stories high, of red or yellow brick and no steel frames, were the worst death traps. During the many months of intensive bombings, an average of 39,000 houses in London were damaged or destroyed per week. In October, 1940, twenty per cent of London's gas users had no gas. During another month there were 8,000 breaks in gas mains. On one day, by sheer freak, many sewers were hit. It took three weeks to remove the disastrous effects. Once, three bombs penetrated forty feet into subway stations. A single bomb cut 58,000 telephone wires. The May 10, 1941, raid killed 1,400 people in London alone. It is not easy to take it.

Sam Herbert, official of the British Embassy in Lisbon, said to me, "You must see my friend Paton. I'll give you a letter to him." That was a happy suggestion. The Reverend William W. Paton is minister of the Victoria Docks Presbyterian Church in West Ham. West Ham is an area of factories, wharves, and docks lying between the Thames River and a vital railroad in east London. Paton showed me his church. Only parts of the concrete floor remain. Block after block, block after block of two-story brick residences has been leveled by bombs. Paton was and is in charge of all the air-raid rescue and precaution work in this vast area. He is the hero, and popular hero, of West Ham. Tales of his vigor and courage during the blitz have become legends. In their worst blitz night they had 100 dead and 450 wounded, out of a total population of 300,000. On that night, and on every raid night, Paton was out in the streets. Factories flew into the air, incendiary bombs dropped in thousands; he went about his business directing salvage work, directing the fire-fighters, comforting the people, taking care of the needs of the homeless and hungry and bereaved.

"A man and a half, a man and a half," Paton's chauffeur repeated as he drove me home after my visit to West Ham. "He will go far after the war." Paton is one of a new corps of people's leaders whom the blitz has moved to the fore. Young at fifty, he has energy, drive, and fight. His sympathies are with Labor, but not with complacent, orthodox Labor.

I asked him whether the people hated the Germans. He said during raids bitterness grew but then it simmered down and died away. The general feeling of the inhabitants was "fatalism without despair."

"Any desire to end the war?" I inquired.

"With victory, yes," he replied.

"What has happened to religion?"

"Nothing," Paton said. "Neither more nor less."

"Have the raids and the war changed ethical standards? Are people looser and more easy-going? Is the attitude 'Oh, well, I might as well have a good time'?"

"No," he replied with certainty. "Standards are completely the same. There is somewhat more drinking because workingmen have more money, but no more drunkenness, and neither more nor less immorality." Morals as usual. I subsequently asked the same questions of others qualified to reply and got similar answers.

On our rounds of the ruins and the well-appointed shelters, two little girls, about thirteen years old, greeted Mr. Paton deferentially. I stopped to talk to them. They had refused to be evacuated from West Ham to the country although the blitz here was as bad as anywhere in Britain.

"Weren't you afraid of the bombs?" I dared to ask.

Their No was a long drawled "Now," and they laughed as though they pitied me. They told me that during the blitz the girls played a game: who could extinguish the most incendiary bombs with the sand from one sandbag. A sandbag weighs about three or four pounds, and the incendiary bombs ignite anything they fall upon and are as big as pineapples. The game was to run around the streets and on roofs while these bombs fell and throw sand on them and count how many you could put out with one bag. The winner of the game put out five.

I asked a woman who had crossed her arms under her bosom what would happen to such girls when they grew up. "They will make sure that they live better than their mothers," she replied.

There is one new cult in wartime Britain, the cult of the common man. Sir Warren Fisher is in charge of civilian defense against air raids in the London metropolitan area. Sixty-two, he retired after a long and brilliant career in the highly important post of chief of Britain's civil service, but came back to be active when the war started. He is an aristocrat, graduate of Winchester, a "public" school like Eton and Harrow, which means that it is a rich man's private school. But he said to me, "England is divided between those who drop their h's—the Cockneys and the under-privileged—and those who don't, and I would rather rely on the former who have conducted themselves marvelously in the raids. The Cockney is made of sturdy stuff even though he hasn't eaten enough most of his life." Several times in this and subsequent conversations Sir Warren stressed his preference. "I'd rather depend on the Cockney than on the folk of Mayfair," he would say.

A high officer of the Royal Air Force said to me, "If it had not been for the ordinary chap we would have been down the drain."

The high priest of the new cult of the common man is J. B. Priestley, well-known British playwright. England seemed to be on her death bed and Priestley came and touched England's soul; that is hard to forget. It was right after Dunkirk in June, 1940. The life of Britain hung by a hair. Britain saved itself by a remarkable effort. Dunkirk is poetry. A miracle took place. A British army was in the maw of Hitler. Englishmen rose up and crossed stormy waters in rowboats, old schooners, yachts, and fishing smacks to rescue soldiers stranded on bomb-pocked beaches. Over three hundred thousand men were withdrawn from Nazi jaws about to close. The nation was in a mood of elation and sacrifice. Men and women worked at their lathes until they fell in exhaustion; England needed arms to repel an invasion. Danger and the triumph over danger had welded the country together as nothing in modern times. Priestley spoke to Britain in that great hour. For ten weeks after Dunkirk, every Sunday evening at 9:20, he went to the British Broadcasting Corporation's microphone and spoke, and the whole nation listened. He became an institution. His voice inspired faith in Britain's ability to survive. His power as a broadcaster rivaled Churchill's. He was not the government. He occupies no official position and never did. He spoke of the people to the people. He spoke for the people. He wants them to live in a better world. He is not a conservative. Neither is he a socialist or communist. He is a populist who believes in the unused talents of the common man and distrusts the tired, soft aristocrats and the hard-boiled merchants who, he says, made such a sorry mess of the business of government. The people should rule, Priestley cries.

What right have the rich, he argues, to the many quiet charming squares inside London from which the public is barred by iron railings? The railings are being taken down to be melted into munitions. That opens the parks to the public. Bravo, shouts Priestley, and he hopes the change is permanent. He lauds the man in the street, the man in the "pub" or beer saloon, the woman over the washboard and the mother in the air-raid shelter. He ridicules the stuffed-shirt Colonel Blimps who do not understand the great things that are happening in the present because they live in the past and therefore cannot be relied upon to build a better future.

The conservatives of Britain did not relish Priestley's weekly broadcasts and wrote angry letters to him which he answered angrily on the air. Their strictures riled him. He could not "take" them. The authorities took him off the air. Maybe the country was getting a bit tired of his preachings. Dunkirk wore off after a while. But it remains in the blood of England, and Priestley, too, remains a popular power.

Priestley's chief goal is a Britain worthy of the men and women who are saving Britain from Hitler, not a Britain with slums, unemployment, derelict areas, and undernourishment. "You have no right to use the real Britain to fight a war," he says in his book, *Out of the People*, "and then announce that you are doing it to preserve a quite different and much less real Britain. This is cheating."

The British are as one in fighting the Nazis. But some, a minority, are also fighting to preserve the old Britain which was very good to them, and some, a majority, are fighting to create a new Britain. In face of the common foreign enemy, the contest at home is restrained. The war abroad has produced an armistice within. But Britain is actually engaged in two wars, a war against the New Order of Hitler and another against the old order of Neville Chamberlain. This happens in every war. In the first world war Prime Minister Lloyd George promised the British "homes for heroes" because it is such promises that make heroes. Later, not enough homes were forthcoming, and that is one reason why England was so reluctant to go to war against Hitler. They had no faith that war would improve things. France fell because it lacked this faith. But now a new faith has been kindled in England. The Britisher believes in himself, in his country, and in a better day. That is the secret of British morale. That is why the British can take it.

Many conservatives, many upper-class people realize that the old England is slowly perishing. I talked in London to Tory members of Parliament and to men who bear titles of nobility and they saw and indeed welcomed the new day that was dawning. "The millions who fight a war," one of them said to me, "must reap the fruits of victory." All this has little to do, as Sir Gerald Campbell truthfully assured an American audience, with "the doctrines of Karl Marx, nor will Britain go 'socialist' in the old-fashioned European sense of the term, which connotes barricades and red flags, yet economic and social equality will inevitably be the aim of post-war Britain." Sir Gerald was specific: "The principle is already being accepted that a citizen of the British democracy is entitled to certain fundamental rights in the economic as well as the political sphere, to a standard of nutrition as well as of freedom, to good housing as well as habeas corpus, to the right to work as well as the right to vote."

The nineteenth century saw a struggle for political democracy. Now life has shown that political democracy unsupported by economic democracy and social security falls a prey to dictatorship. Hitler is not merely an aggressor. He does not merely clap innocent folk in jail and torture non-German races. He challenges capitalism. He challenges democracy. He says, "We are better than you." He has won his many victories against democracies and within democracies because capitalism and democracy are imperfect. Millions in Britain have grasped this. To beat Hitler the British must be stronger but they must also be better. They must answer his challenge by setting their own house in order. "Social security must be the first object of our domestic policy after the war," Foreign Minister Eden promised in a speech on May 29, 1941.

Eden, the young Conservative, Priestley, the populist, H. G. Wells, the architect of crystal utopias, and Harold J. Laski, the socialist, are creating a new social climate in Britain. But Churchill and Halifax and Beaverbrook also make their contributions to another climate, and sometimes the wind blows hot and sometimes cold. There is never a cyclone, rarely even a gale; usually there is only a mild breeze and occasionally complete calm. Nobody knows what can happen after the war. But most open-eyed observers are sure that something will happen. This is as near as England has got to revolution. Journals like *The New Statesman*, *The Tribune*, and *The Economist* lay down a weekly barrage of constructive criticism against the government. The daily press also takes shots at the Cabinet. Parliament serves as a sounding board for the nation and as a vent for popular displeasure. War acts as a checkrein, not as a muzzle. The Labor Party is in the government—which helps the government. The state collects all war profits from business. The trade unions have given up many privileges won during decades of hard battles with employers. An official truce has called off the struggle of parties and groups at home. But everybody is thinking of the day when the end of the foreign war will end the domestic armistice; and most interests are jockeying for good positions in the future.

"Do you think it possible," a young pilot said to me standing by his Hurricane pursuit plane, "that we shall be unemployed when it is all over?" He was not sure. He was puzzled and worried. Above all, England fears post-war unemployment; people want to work. They have seen slum houses fall on them and crumble under them. They want good homes. They have seen tired, old men with no imagination lead them to disaster, just as Churchill and Labor and the Liberals had predicted. They want wiser leaders who are of and for the people. That is all.

Meanwhile, the British people work loyally and wait patiently and do not press their case with vigor. "There is a war on," they say. During my sojourn in England I spent a week in the industrial area of Yorkshire. All doors were opened for me by William Dobbie, a Labor member of Parliament from Yorkshire whom I have known for many years. The Lord Mayor of York—normal population, 100,000, now swollen to 120,000—led me down into the basement of the city hall and joyfully pointed to forty-nine five-pound parcels of bacon, milk, butter, tea, and sugar just received from York Village, Maine, and York Harbor, Maine, for distribution among the needy. "Here's one from Miss Catharine Marshall," the Lord Mayor exclaimed. Then he showed me a list, carved in marble, of the Lord

Mayors of York since 1217. An attendant in diplomatic dress took the city's most ancient treasures out of the cupboards and set them on a huge table so I could see them. There was the studded sword, dated 1439, which belonged to the Emperor Sigismund, father-in-law of King Richard II, a gold chain of office still worn by the Lord Mayor on ceremonial functions which weighs one pound four and a half ounces and was wrought in 1603, a gold loving cup—26 ounces of pure gold—made in 1672, and so on and so on. After this inspection, I was left alone to look around in the library of the city hall. I made notes from *The History of York*, in two volumes, written by Francis Drake, and published in London on August 1, 1736.

The roar of a bomber overhead jerked me out of ancient history. Outside on the street, soldiers in khaki, military trucks, women carrying gas masks and "To The Trenches" signs re-established the present for me. But that excursion into history had said, "There will always be an England."

Forty years ago a great British social scientist, Seebohm Rowntree, wrote *Poverty*, a study of conditions in York. In 1936, he began a second survey of the same ground. It took him and his assistants five years to sift, tabulate, digest, and write up the data, and his second book on York was only published in 1941. He calls it *Poverty and Progress*. There has been progress. There has been progress everywhere, for this is a century of invention, mechanical advance, and cheaper and more goods for the people. York's death rate fell from 17.2 per thousand in 1899 to 11.6 in 1936. Only 55 babies in every thousand die now compared with 161 forty years ago. Housing and social services have improved too. But Mr. Rowntree, surveying existing conditions, finds that "nearly half the children born in working-class families will have lived below the level of dietetic and health efficiency during the first and critical five years of their lives." The birth rate in York has been halved during the last forty years. In 1936, 43 per cent of all children under 14 in York were in "poor families."

Poverty and Progress appeared while England was deeply engaged in a war for its existence, yet the book made a profound impression on a wide public. There will always be an England. But what kind?

From York I went to visit steel plants and munitions factories in several northern English cities. (The authorities asked me not to mention their names lest the Nazis, by a subtle combination of facts, learn where the factories are.) Labor and capital work in smooth collaboration. In one plant I sat in the board of directors' room with the managing director and the leading trade unionist of the region. Bewhiskered Englishmen looked down on us from faded oils and darkened frames; they were the managers of the plant in generations gone by. We were having tea and buttered toast. The managing director recalled the first world war. He recalled an occasion when David Lloyd George went to Glasgow to talk to striking workingmen and they howled him off the platform. "That would be inconceivable now," he commented. Strikes then were numerous and virulent; now they are completely insignificant. Everybody wants to defeat Hitler; the workingmen would do more than they are doing. Over the teacups, the trade unionist nodded assent to everything the managing director said, and when the trade unionist spoke the managing director nodded assent.

Every town and village in Britain has its Home Guard and they all form a national Home Guard operating under the control of the army. In case of invasion, they will defend their homes while the army meets the enemy on the beaches and then on the battlefield. If the enemy drops parachutists, the Home Guard will "account for them" in its own locality. "Account for them?" a Home Guard said to me in Yorkshire. "We'll chew them up. Let them come."

Workingmen in factories and clerks in offices now often work up to ten hours a day. Yet after work they train in the Home Guard. There are over a million of them throughout the country. For two days I walked around a town, went into plants, homes, shelters, hospitals, fire stations. On the evening of the second day, I saw men hurrying to the outskirts. They were in khaki uniform and some carried rifles. I had seen them at lathes and ledgers. Now they were going out to the Home Guard headquarters to train as soldiers. They were below or above the age of military service, or, as was the case with most of them, they were in "reserved occupations," which means that their occupation was so important—making guns, tanks, ammunition—that they were not drafted by the army.

The lieutenant colonel in charge was the secretary of a member of Parliament. The member of Parliament was a private, or volunteer, taking orders from the lieutenant colonel. Factory managers march beside their errand boys, all eager, all serious. For "he" may invade, they say. And if "he" doesn't, it will be because he knows the quality of the Home Guard. "We know every road and tree and rock in the neighborhood," they said to me. "We could cut the Germans to pieces." Being mechanics and laborers they improvise weapons; they get an old motorcycle, cover it with armor, and screw a machine gun into the sidecar. A truck becomes an armored car. They make their own amateur flame-throwers.

I watched a Home Guard battalion line up for rifle drill. Then it marched off to a nearby meadow to practice signaling, stretcher-bearing, hand-grenade throwing, and Tommy-gun shooting. A moment later I followed up to the meadow. I stopped where a man was filling in holes in the road. He straightened out.

"How old are you?" I asked.

"Dooble six," he replied in a queer Yorkshire accent. Sixty-six! More questions elicited this information: As a boy of thirteen, he had gone to dig coal in a mine. He has been working at the coal face ever since—for fifty-three years. His friends calculated that he had spent thirty years of his life in darkness. I was curious, since I have never been in a coal mine and never want to go into one, to know how he dug coal. He sat down on the side of his foot and lowered his head till his right cheek was about two feet from the ground. Then he made horizontal motions with both hands as though he held a pick. He had done that for eight hours today, as he did every day. An hour ago, he returned home. He had removed some of the coal dust from his face—there were still smudge spots on his nose and chin—had eaten his dinner, and now he was filling in the holes in the road so that the Home Guards would have an easier path to their training field. He laughed a lot, showing toothless gums, and his only complaint about the war was that the beer had deteriorated in strength.

"Well," he said, ending our conversation, "I have to get on with my job. I'm digging Hitler's grave."

I spent the next evening and night at the house of the Dobbies in York. William Dobbie, a former railwayman and ex-president of the National Union of Railwaymen, types all his own letters—at the age of sixty—and answers and investigates the complaints made in every letter he gets. Mrs. Dobbie keeps house and makes it a house beautiful. It is one of a row of small cottages each surrounded by gardens. But Dobbie never had more than a nodding acquaintance with his middle-class neighbors.

This evening, however, he went out to talk to the man next door who was on ARP duty for the night. Dobbie told him he was keeping his clothes on that night and would be ready if called. I listened while both of them talked and then the man turned to me and said, "One virtue of this war is that it has brought English people closer to one another. Our homes stand and fall and burn together." He went off on his rounds. I noticed everywhere in England that the British had discovered one another. They had behaved well in the air raids. That had given them an added faith in themselves. The British had always possessed a sense of effortless superiority. Appeasement and Chamberlain had knocked it on the head. It was back now. No sane person will again call the British decadent.

All evening heavy planes hummed in the black sky. I went out into the street to see how much I could see. Occasionally, I could discern dark moving shapes up above. But usually my ears were a better guide. The big planes approached separately from several angles and converged into a group not far beyond the house. They were eastbound, going to bomb Germany.

To bomb Germany, and particularly Berlin, is the most popular thing the British government can do. "Give him back some of what he's given us."

I returned into the house and played with the radio dial. I found some good music and let it stay on. Mrs. Dobbie tapped out the rhythm with her foot. Dobbie listened with pleasure. Then a deep voice said in German, "This is Breslau." Lord Haw Haw, the English fascist who broadcasts for the Nazis, could not speak tonight, the announcer stated, but his deputy would continue his lectures on Winston Churchill. In words of vituperation and abuse, the speaker discussed the career and character of the British Prime Minister. Mrs. Dobbie fumed, but Dobbie laughed, and they both agreed that this made everybody angry and convinced nobody.

The night was quiet. It was dawn when the drone of aeroplane motors awakened me. I looked at my watch: four o'clock. The British bombers were returning from Germany.

At breakfast, Mrs. Dobbie told of the son of a neighborhood merchant who had piloted a bomber to Germany and never come back. "And a very fine lad. Some German lads have been shot down around here too."

Often, German airmen bail out over Britain and are taken to hospital for medical treatment. When the women of the vicinity hear of it they ransack their libraries and attics for old German books, or French books, and bring them to the enemy patients. Sometimes, British women cook special food at home for German prisoners in hospitals. RAF pilots told me that occasionally, after shooting down a German airman in England, they go to visit him in hospital and give him gifts.

It is difficult to wage a war the way the British people are doing it; they do it out of necessity without ferocity. They have a will to win without the wish to hate. It is difficult—and very civilized.

FIGHTER PILOTS

3. FIGHTER PILOTS

By arrangement with Jack I went down by train to G. to visit his aerodrome. Jack, six-feet-four and forty, resplendent in the uniform of an RAF flying officer, met me at the railway station. "This is my commanding officer," he said indicating the young man at his side. His commanding officer, Dan, was five-feet-five and twenty-six. Dan had chestnut hair, a lithe body, smiling eyes, and an animated face. I deposited my bag in a small hotel and then we went to another hotel to dine. We were overjoyed when the waitress consented to give us a second portion of canned pineapple for dessert.

After dinner we dashed out to the airport, Dan driving like a rocket in his tiny dull-camouflaged car. Apropos of something he said, I remarked, "Well, you're England's glamor boys." To which he replied, "Yeah? The life of a pilot consists of months of boredom interspersed with moments of fear."

It was dark when we passed the sentry and rolled on to the airfield. Without even entering the squadron's hut, Dan took me over to his own Hurricane fighter plane. We climbed up on the wing and he proudly showed me the fifteen little yellow swastikas on the left side of the fuselage. He had brought down "fifteen Jerries" since the war started, ten confirmed, five probable. "But we count the probables as sure," he commented. "I'm sure anyway." We bent over into the cockpit and Dan explained some of the hundred and one gadgets which every pilot must understand and manipulate. He moved the sights and found the range. It was astonishing that anyone flying at great height, at great speed, and in great danger, could operate these crowded handles, valves, levers, and buttons. This new Hurricane has four cannon mounted so that they converge on one target. When the aviator presses a cap near the rudder all the cannon fire at once and the bullets emerge from the front edge of the wings. Dan showed me the cap. It is about two inches in diameter and reacts to the slightest touch. The plane never carries more than ten seconds' ammunition. If the pilot put his finger on the cap and held it there for one-sixth of a minute all his ammunition would be gone. I was surprised. Dan explained that he could bring down four or five enemy machines with ten seconds of ammunition. It sufficed for several battles in the air. A burst of firing is just one touch of the cap. Dan said he taught his pilots to treat the cap as though it were a red-hot stove: apply a finger lightly to it and if your foe is inside your sights he is doomed. Ten seconds of ammunition is a very heavy load, and no effective fighting plane could carry more. The cannon shoot at a fantastic speed. The plane flies at 360 to 385 miles an hour.

We went inside the wooden hut where the pilots stay when waiting for orders to rush on to the field and take their planes up. Dan introduced me to about eight men, officers and sergeants, one sergeant a recent arrival from Canada. Their ages ranged from 22 to 29. Wallie, son of a rich merchant who traded with South America, was twenty-nine and the veteran of the squadron. On the wooden walls were two seductive prints from *Esquire* and a photograph of a demure British film actress. But most of the space was covered with complicated diagrams of British, German, and Italian aircraft. Every pilot must know the machines in his own air force so as not to attack them and the machines of the enemy so as to know where to attack them and how to avoid their fire. He must know what are the vulnerable spots in the Messerschmitt 109F, the most formidable German pursuit plane, and he must know the position of its weapons, the position of its pilot, its speed, and its maneuverability. Whenever an enemy plane is brought down, British technicians take it apart and study its every detail. Where is the armor thinnest? What are the blind spots from which an opponent can be hit? This information is sent to all aerodromes.

Dan's squadron members were lounging around either on bunks in a neighboring room or in chairs in the office. Each man had an open locker stuffed with the things he must quickly put on before taking off to fight. In cold weather they first dress in a fur zipper jacket, fur trousers, and fur boots. On top of that they wear their "Mae West," a yellow rubber sleeveless jacket which is inflated by a mechanical device so that the front swells out into round bulbs. The back also fills up. From the collar of this jacket hangs a yellow cape. In the pockets are bags of red or green powder. If a pilot bails out over the sea the "Mae West" keeps him afloat; the cape lies on the water to make him more visible to an aeroplane searching for him, and the powder dissolves and creates a big spot of bright color on the water which likewise adds to visibility. Dan put on the "Mae West" and took out of another of its pockets a little yellow skull cap with a string which goes around the chin. This serves the same purpose of aiding the searchers. Above the "Mae West," the pilot wears a parachute. Its harness goes around his chest and between his legs. He sits on the folded parachute. Fastened to the folded parachute is a rubber boat or dinghy which opens easily and fills with air. The pilot sits in it on the water while hoping for rescue.

The last item the pilot puts on is his soft leather helmet fitted with inside earphones. From the helmet two pipes hang like a girl's plaits. In the plane the pilot plugs one of these into a socket. That is for receiving and sending radio messages. He plugs in the second whenever he needs oxygen. The helmet is a highly complicated affair, hiding more than it reveals.

By the time the pilot has got into all these clothes, mechanics have started his motors by a secret device on the ground; without a moment's delay the airman hops into the cockpit and mounts into the air.

On a tier of lockers stood a cage occupied by a parrot. They had saved it from a bombed-out house in a nearby city. Its vocabulary consisted of "Bugger" and "Go to bed."

I asked the pilots about food. They said they ate

enough and well. Jack said they missed only fruit. Dan told us he bought peaches at four shillings and sixpence —ninety cents—apiece. Wallie reported that he had purchased a bunch of grapes the other day and calculated that each grape cost him fourpence—seven cents. The boys laughed, the parrot said "Bugger," and the boys laughed again.

They brought in some Hurricane ammunition. It came in bands and the men carrying it showed how heavy it was. The shells are twenty millimeters thick— about an inch. Each bullet is a formidable creature. Dan held one against the bullet of a machine gun which used to be the Hurricane's armament. It was like a Great Dane beside a puppy. On the band, the bullets alternate; the first is a solid steel pellet which pierces armor. It is followed by high explosive and incendiary bullets which enter through the perforation. Then come another steel hole-driller and more explosives and incendiaries.

Cruising, while looking for quarry, the Hurricane can stay in the air an hour and a half. But if involved in continual combat it has gasoline for only 45 to 50 minutes' flight. The pilots love their machines and swear that there are none better in the world. The crews of the Spitfires say the same about their planes. The Spitfire and the Hurricane, both pursuit ships, look very much alike. Jack says they belong to the same species, the Spitfire being the female—more elegant and lighter —while the Hurricane is the thick-set male.

London argues on the necessity of the black-out. Some of my friends contend that it could be abandoned or relaxed. I asked Dan what he thought. He said he had flown over London during the night at a height of 15,000 feet, and even at such an altitude he could see light streaming out of a single open door. He said the black-out of German cities was more perfect than in England. Any kind of light helped the bomber overhead, and he thought the black-out ought to be tightened rather than abandoned. "But," he added, "the real purpose of the black-out is to keep the people at home. If the streets were normally lighted in the evening they would be as full of pedestrians and cars as in peacetime, and in case of a raid everybody would rush for shelter and there would be confusion. The blackout keeps people at home and widely distributed over the city instead of congregated in central amusement areas."

The very cordial atmosphere which prevailed in the room prompted me to ask Dan and Wallie, who were officers, whether any barrier separated them from the sergeants. Would they go into town and have dinner with sergeants? They replied that there was no distinction between men who fly. The distinction was rather between pilots and ground crews. Dan said he was more likely to associate with a pilot sergeant than with an officer who did not fly. "Generally speaking," Dan declared, rather proudly, "there are no social distinctions in the RAF. We are not like the army where men, NCO's, and officers are kept strictly apart. We are not formal in the RAF. We cannot march. In the army they think they can win the war by forming threes. It used to be fours; remember? Now, they're down to marching in threes. That's the progress the bloody army has made. My squadron would never get anywhere if we had to march there." The men enjoyed this and laughed. "The army doesn't like us," the squadron commander continued. "We're too young"—and after a pause—"we do too much."

Food was brought in, first sandwiches and then tea and stew. Nobody drank alcohol. Wallie amused us and nonplussed me for half an hour with amazing card tricks. Jack then drove me back into town.

When I awoke at 8:30 next morning, the maid brought me a pitcher of hot water for washing and shaving. Under my window a soldier whistled "Yes, My Darling Daughter," this war's most popular marching song. In the last war, it was "It's a Long Way to Tipperary" or "Pack Up Your Troubles in Your Old Kit Bag."

At breakfast, the waitress said, "Take some more sugar. I'm not looking."

I waited for Dan's car. The girl at the desk talked philosophy. She was experiencing a private tragedy and wanted to talk about it. I listened gladly.

Jack and Dan met me at the airfield and we entered Jack's office. Jack is adjutant of the squadron. On his desk stood a little silver loving cup. They told me its history: "At dawn, one gray March day, a giant bomber circled over the aerodrome and dropped lower and lower. Now, bombers do not belong on fighter aerodromes. So the alarm was sounded and the guns manned. The bomber descended and finally landed. We went out, cautiously, revolvers at the ready, to investigate.

When the bomber came to a halt, the pilot rose in his cockpit and exclaimed in a deep guttural accent, 'Vee arr von Hamburg,' at which we stepped back and prepared for a fight. It turned out that this was the Polish crew of a new British bomber. They had spent the night bombing Hamburg and had lost their way on the return journey. They were welcomed and feted, and several days after their departure they sent this cup with the following inscription:

> *To charmy down*
> *Where we came down*
> *A Polish crew*
> *Says 'Here's to You.'*"

On Jack's door is chalked up the squadron's record of achievement. Since the war they have destroyed 133½ enemy planes, probably destroyed 47 more, and damaged 42. One-half is granted for a machine shot down in conjunction with a pilot from another squadron. As soon as a pilot returns from combat he reports to the squadron's intelligence officer, who questions him and decides with him what the result of the fight has been. The intelligence officer tends to be on the conservative side and insists on clear testimony. Sometimes he credits the pilot with only a probable; later the coastal command or a destroyer on duty confirms that the "probable" has been fished out of the sea, and then the pilot crows with delight.

I was allowed to read a batch of written reports which the pilots are required to make as soon as they land. I copied one that Dan wrote during the Battle of Britain in the summer of 1940 when these young men held the fate of England in their hands. Dan led his whole squadron—twelve planes—into the air one afternoon, and at 5:45 P.M. he encountered eighty enemy fighters seven miles south of the English coast. They were Messerschmitt 110's and 109's, the latter carrying two machine guns and a cannon, operating at a height of between 13,000 and 7,000 feet. On sighting the Nazis, Dan climbed towards the sun, his men in their Hurricanes behind him. Then it was every man for himself. This is what Dan reported: "I dived, unseen by enemy aircraft, out of the sun and attacked an ME 110. I gave him two short bursts at 250 yards and he caught fire. Then I climbed again and dived vertically at another ME 110. We fought at fifty to three hundred yards from one another. I got in a two-second burst and his starboard engine was enveloped in flames and he broke away from his formation.

"I then climbed a third time and started chasing the main enemy formation towards France in company with two ME 109's. I mistook them for Hurricanes. They turned to attack me. One did a head-on attack, the other went for my tail. At ten yards, I fired a three-second burst at the engine and under-surface of the plane attacking head-on and went into a spin vertically downwards. One enemy machine followed parallel with me. I pulled out of the dive at 4,000 feet and hid in a cloud. The enemy lost me. I came home."

Dan scored one point for an ME 110 destroyed and one-half for a probable. The other members of his team recorded a second ME destroyed and one damaged. British casualties in that fray were two planes lost. One pilot who parachuted over the sea was missing, a second was picked up wounded. The battle had lasted four minutes.

All mechanics, repair men, and armorers of the squadron were training to defend the aerodrome in case of enemy attack, and so Jack summoned a truckload of them and we drove off to a shooting range to practice with American Tommy guns. They love the Tommy guns and expressed the hope that the United States would send more. The magazine holds twenty rounds which are discharged at an unbelievably rapid rate. Each man emptied a magazine; they let me do the same.

On the way down to the rifle range I was sitting with Jack and the driver. We passed along the entire length of the aerodrome. It had been a vast farm, but was now leveled and many parts had been paved. It has huge buildings, hangars, repair shops, on it. It has underground storerooms, expensive guns for protection against air attack, a new water supply, large mess halls, kitchens, and houses for the crews to sleep in. Its personnel probably numbered 700 men and women altogether. The cost of transforming the farm into an aerodrome must have been enormous. The cost of maintenance is enormous. We estimated that there must be one thousand such aerodromes in Great Britain. What a tremendous outlay of money and materials for war.

"I suppose," I said, "if the war continues for two years your government will find the money to run the war?" Jack nodded affirmatively.

"But if the war ended after the two years and there were need of building a school or clearing a slum, the authorities would plead shortage of money?" Jack nodded again.

"Yet if the war were to continue for a third year the government would be able to finance the war in the third year, too?" Jack nodded.

The other men had listened and when we alighted at the rifle range they took it up. "That was always true," a Scot said. "Money to burn to pay for killing people. No money to keep people alive and happy."

"Things must be different after this war," several of them said.

"What can you do about it?" I inquired.

Nobody knew. They smoked and pushed one another around and waited eagerly for their turn to use the Tommy gun.

We went to the officers' mess for lunch. Girls in RAF uniform served the meal. The hall was bright and airy, the food good, and the conversation intelligent. After dessert we adjourned to a large lounge for talk and coffee. Someone turned on the radio and got Lord Haw Haw broadcasting in English from Germany. Three or four pilots came nearer to the radio, listened for a moment, laughed, and turned him off. He had told them that in last night's raids over Germany the British lost twenty per cent of the machines used. But they knew, because they were on the inside of the RAF, that the losses had been only five per cent. What was the point of listening to more drivel?

Dan introduced me to his superior officer, Group

Captain M. The captain asked me whether I would like to go up for a flight. I saw no sense in just flying for flying's sake, but it would have taken more courage to say No than to accept. So I said, "Of course." The captain authorized Dan to take me up in his training plane, a "Maggie"—Magister.

Before taking off, Dan wanted to show me his squadron's billet. It was a beautiful mansion built like a castle with a turret. The halls and rooms were oak-paneled and spacious in the tradition of the British nobility. The grounds were well-kept with sunken rose gardens and tall box bushes cut into odd shapes. Upstairs there were numerous rooms and bathrooms.

I asked Dan about the owner. "Oh," he replied, "he owns coal mines."

"Good break for you fellows," I said.

"Don't you think we ought to have the best?" he smiled.

I did.

They had four tennis courts, and they played every day. I asked Jack whether he still played hockey and cricket. He replied affirmatively.

"Do you play cricket in white flannels?" I asked.

"Of course," he laughed. "You don't think one plays cricket in blue overalls. It wouldn't be cricket."

Dan had an open typewriter in his room with a sheet of paper in it. "Author?" I asked him.

He confessed. He was writing his autobiography. He had been a medical student, the son of a physician. Before the war he had owned a sailboat in which he used to cross the Channel on visits to France. He had learned to fly in a sports plane several years before the war and had volunteered for the RAF in 1938.

"The book helps me a lot," he mused. "It's creative, constructive. I would hate to think that my life was entirely devoted to killing."

Jack had placed a bowl of roses on the mantelpiece of his room. The windowsill was stacked high with books on economics by conservative authorities and also by Karl Marx and Lenin. We discussed Hemingway's *For Whom the Bell Tolls*. Dan said he had not been interested in politics before 1938 and had not followed the events of the Spanish civil war. But he now knew how badly the British government had let down the Spanish Republic and Czechoslovakia.

We drove over to the squadron's hut, and Dan busied himself preparing the "Maggie" for our flight. It was the maddest thing I have ever done.

Dan announced before we left that he had arranged a rendezvous with Wallie and Bobbie over the sea. I didn't quite understand what that meant. The "Maggie" was tuning up. I watched Wallie. He was on the field playing with a model aeroplane made of thick orange-colored paper. He would wind up the propeller with his fingers, release the plane, and watch its antics as it rose, dived, floated for a brief space, and fell to earth. Then he would run across the aerodrome to pick it up and wind it again.

When the "Maggie" was ready, they started to find a parachute for me. Most of them were too small. Finally, by stooping somewhat, I managed to wriggle into one. The men hoisted me on to the wing and I climbed into the cockpit. I was wearing an ordinary suit, no coat, no hat. I sat down on the folded parachute which made a soft cushion. They strapped me in with three straps and fastened them together with a linch pin right over my breastbone.

"Now," Dan said to me, "in case of accident you open the bolt in the little door here so that you can step out on the wing more easily. Then pull the linch pin. That loosens you from the plane. Next, get out on the wing and jump. When you are clear of the plane pull this with your right hand," and he indicated a steel handle on the left side of the belt of the parachute.

"Is that the ripcord?" I asked.

Yes, it was.

"Remember three things," Bobbie repeated. "Unbolt the door. Pull the pin. Pull the ripcord. All right?"

I motioned that I was ready. Dan sat in a tight cockpit in front of me. Both cockpits were open. The plane was tiny with short wings. The motor whirled, the plane ran along the runway for a short stretch, and then Dan lifted it abruptly off the ground. We rose steeply. Dan turned his head around, held up one of his hands with the thumb up, and looked inquiringly at me. I held a thumb up. He shook his head approvingly.

Of a sudden the motor stopped, Dan turned his face to me, shouted "Bristol," and indicated the city below us. At the moment I was not much interested in geographical data and would rather have heard the sound of the motor than the name of the town. I tried to convey that idea to Dan by violent circular motions of my hands. By that time the motor was on again.

The wind howled past my ears and blew hair about. In front of me Dan, hatless too, was patting the back of his head to keep his hair in position. He leaned down to look at the instruments, looked to either side, and then started smoothing his hair again. I had given up the effort and let my hair fly in the wind.

Presently Dan held up both his hands and turned his face to me and smiled. I motioned to him to take hold of the controls. I thought he was showing me that the plane could fly without him. But I wanted no fancy demonstrations.

Altitude 3,000 feet. I felt very cold. The wind roared in my ears, tore at my hair, and burned my face. We were in a cloud, and water was running down the windshields. Up and up we went. It got still colder. My teeth began to chatter and I was not quite sure whether it was from cold or fear. Anyway I would have been happy to see the sun or the earth. I suspected that the motor was not working too well. I listened. It kept saying, "Uh-uh, uh-uh, uh-uh," and my heart echoed, "Uh-uh, uh-uh, uh-uh."

Dan was biting his fingernails. That disturbed me. Dan looked up, looked to both sides, looked downward. He was looking for a place to make a forced landing, I decided. "The bolt, the pin, the ripcord," I rehearsed. Dan lowered the nose of the "Maggie" and descended steeply. Houses and farms appeared. We were out of the cloud. The motor sang again.

The sea. I studied the fortifications on the beach.

This is where the British would first meet invading Nazis. Dan banked sharply. That meant he tipped one wing so that the plane was almost vertical. I hoped the sea would not hit us. He circled several times and then pointed; the huge hulk of a Hurricane came into view.

"Wallie," Dan shouted.

Wallie waved. I saw his face distinctly. Then he mounted and flew away. Dan showed me something on the water below. Wallie had dropped a small smoke bomb which seemed to me about two inches in diameter. Suddenly, Wallie opened his throttle and with a fearful noise dived towards the water, his cannon blazing away full force. He shot out the smoke bomb and it disappeared.

Dan banked again and circled some more. He pointed. "Bobbie."

There was the second Hurricane. Bobbie came in between us and Wallie, dropped a smoke bomb, and flew away to get in position for a dive. Then something strange happened. Wallie let his plane twist downward. Would he crash into the sea? Instead he again opened fire with his cannon and smashed Bobbie's target so that when Bobbie dived there was nothing in the water to aim at.

Dan was laughing and smoothing the hair on the back of his head.

We had trouble returning. We had a tail wind of fierce power which tugged and tore at the plane and at us. "Maggie" behaved badly. She skipped and looped all over the place. Dan ate more fingernail. I was alternately cold and very hot, and looked at my watch, and tried to find landmarks that would indicate we were nearer home. In the end, we landed.

When I got out of the "Maggie," Wallie, who had returned before us because his Hurricane was much faster than the Magister, was again running after his orange-colored paper plane. He told us with much laughter that Bobbie had not enjoyed his prank of knocking out the second smoke bomb. But when Bobbie turned up it was obvious that he had been reconciled to his loss. In retrospect, at tea in the big officers' mess, my flight to the sea and back seemed a delightful adventure, and I was glad I hadn't refused to go.

Dan said he was a bit worried when we were in the cloud. The motor functioned poorly.

Dan and Jack drove me back to town and to the railway station. I asked Dan what he would do when the war ended. "Take a three years' trip around the world," he answered. "Go to America. Sleep."

All of England will be tired.

London was black when I arrived. The lights were small, dim, and blue. I groped my way into a taxi and went home to dine.

LONDON SPEAKING

4. LONDON SPEAKING

The British Broadcasting Corporation invited me to broadcast in German to Germany. The idea of sitting in London, in a room fifty feet under the ground, helping to bridge the gap between two worlds set to destroy one another was very exciting. Two small microphones placed on a wooden table covered with green cloth were the instruments which worked the miracle.

First, the announcer, a German refugee speaking German, read the news of the day, stressing the places which the RAF had bombed the previous night. Then I spoke in German for seven minutes. My script had been approved by the official censor.

What I said is interesting only because the censor let me say it. I said: "The democracies have learned from the mistakes which they committed in Paris in 1919. There will be no second Versailles Treaty. . . . After Hitler's defeat there may, at first, be no peace conference or peace treaty. . . . In America and in England, there is no thought of imposing reparations on Germany as after the first world war. . . . The democracies have benefited by the past. Not so the Nazis. This time the democracies must give the world a just peace, an enduring peace."

Then the announcer came back to the microphone

and related this incident: A Nazi pilot was shot down over England. He was taken to hospital in a wounded condition. He needed a blood transfusion. Despite his critical state he said he did not wish his blood polluted by non-Aryan blood. So they brought to his bedside three tall blond Englishmen of noble Anglo-Saxon lineage who were ready to give him their blood. The Nazi refused. "No," he said. "I want only German Aryan blood." And he died.

"What does the German mother think of this?" the announcer asked. In German, the definite article also designates one of a group, and *"Die deutsche Mutter"* can mean any German mother. But it can also mean the mother of the pilot.

"What does the German mother think of this?" he asked. "Listen."

A German woman stepped over to the microphone. Beginning slowly in mournful tones she soon rose to a crescendo of shattering emotion. "I am the German mother," she exclaimed. "I bore this boy in hardship. He was suckled at my breast. I gave my last crust of bread to him that he might be strong. He is my flesh."

By this time she was shaking her fists past her ears in ever-faster rhythm. "Now he is dead in London. I would have given him gladly to die for our country. But he did not die for Germany. He was killed by an attachment to Hitler's insane ideas about blood and soil. Hitler has taken our children away from us. My boy might have lived. But he would not be saved. The Nazis had poisoned him with their barbarous philosophy. Give us back our sons, you madman," she shouted.

Again the announcer in cool voice: "You will now hear the names of the German prisoners taken by the British in recent days." This is why Germany listens to the BBC. The announcer read the name of a German U-boat sailor. He gave the sailor's home address in Hamburg. "He is safe in England. He is unhurt. You may write to him. If his mother is not listening in tell her that her son is well." More names and addresses. Hans Laube of such-and-such a street and house number in Bremen, shot down over England, "has got through his operation and is convalescing. He sends greetings to his wife and little daughter." This continued until the end of the half-hour period. "We will be with you again on the same wavelength this evening at six with more news and more names of prisoners."

Germans are executed or given long prison sentences for listening to foreign broadcasts. Still they listen. The British can listen to Germany as much as they please. Churchill is sure of the British. A democracy is stronger because it hears both sides and then acts as though there were only one.

From the BBC building I rushed over, late, to the Savoy Hotel where the P. E. N.—international writers' and artists' organization—was inaugurating its annual congress with a luncheon in honor of the foreign diplomats stationed in London. The vast ballroom was filled with some seven hundred people sitting around large tables packed close together. Among those at my table were Viola Meynell and Sir Sydney Cockerell, former curator of the Fitzwilliam Museum at Cambridge University. He had been an intimate friend of John Ruskin, Britain's great literary critic and philosopher.

The Honorable George Peel, also at the table, leaned over between courses and said, "Sir Sydney, my name is George Peel. I once visited Ruskin."

Sir Sydney, a dignified gray-haired gentleman, replied, "It is most unusual nowadays to have two people at one gathering who had known Ruskin. You must have been a mere boy." Peel declared he had once seen Ruskin with the present Archbishop of Canterbury. Sir Sydney thought he went him one better when he recalled that he had once been with Ruskin and Robert Browning. The conversation moved for a while in the realms of poetry and criticism. Later they asked me some questions about America, and several of my neighbors said they were pleased that America was helping so much. Viola Meynell regretted that a man like Lord Halifax represented England in Washington, D. C. A British Winant would be preferable.

The official proceedings opened when a broad-shouldered functionary of the Savoy, in bright red cutaway coat and stiff white shirt, lifted his voice and cried, "My lords, ladies and gentlemen, I pray silence for a toast to His Majesty, the King."

Everybody arose, wine glass in hand, and said, "The King."

A man in the uniform of an army major who stood at a nearby table said, "The King, God bless him."

Then the same broad-shouldered, silver-voiced functionary shouted, "My lords, ladies and gentlemen, I pray silence for Madame, the chairman," whereupon Margaret Storm Jameson got up and spoke movingly about what England was fighting for.

She then introduced John G. Winant. The audience applauded loudly and all stood. When the ovation ended, the broad-shouldered functionary, spreading his arms wide, exclaimed, "My lords, ladies and gentlemen, I pray silence for His Excellency, the Ambassador of the United States." More applause. I noticed that even those who had never seen Winant before liked him immediately and were impelled to say so. His appearance predisposes people in his favor. His head has a beautiful profile. He is tall, awkward, and shy, and the first reaction of many people is—"Lincoln." He makes an instantaneous impression of honesty and integrity. He spoke about two minutes. For a few seconds he talked extemporaneously and he broke down in the middle of his sentences just as he does in personal conversation. Then he read from his notes. What he said was simple indeed: this war was for those who cared about the important things in life. The audience approved lustily.

The Savoy functionary once more engaged in vocal fanfare for "Madame, the chairman" and Storm Jameson introduced J. B. Priestley, noted British author and playwright. He looks like an average Englishman. But he speaks brilliantly. His task was to propose a toast in honor of the guest of honor, Winant, and also of the other diplomats. Speaking of Winant, he said, "It's interesting how nicely the Americans adjust themselves to us. When we had Chamberlain they sent us Kennedy." There he stopped and everybody understood and laughed. It was a compliment to Winant and a compliment to Churchill. At one point in his remarks, Priestley raised his voice and said, "Do you hear me. I don't know whether I'm speaking or broadcasting. If I'm broadcasting they'll soon cut me off." This reference to his break with the BBC was much appreciated. But he occasionally does broadcast for foreign consumption. And depending on the mood of the people he may return to the microphone. Priestley apologized in his speech for not having time to mention all the ambassadors and ministers present but he did wish to pronounce one name, "the envoy of a gallant country, Ivan Maisky." Maisky got a big hand.

After the meeting broke up I stood around chatting with Arthur Koestler, Kingsley Martin, Storm Jameson, Erika Mann, and others.

At 6 P.M., I went to the home of Countess Moura Boudberg. Bruce Lockhart devotes many pages of *British Agent* to her life in Moscow in 1918. She is an Ukrainian, a very interesting, vital person who has held men like Maxim Gorki and H. G. Wells under her spell. Desmond MacCarthy was there, famous Irish literary critic, Erika Mann, Nancy Cunard of the shipping family, Louise Morgan, special contributor to the London daily *News Chronicle*, H. G. Wells, and Rose Macaulay. Wells arrived with Rose Macaulay. He thinks and lambasts the authorities while Mr. Britling sees it through again. He came in, was handed a whisky and soda, and sat alone. I went over and engaged Rose Macaulay in conversation. She is tall and lean and the skin of her face is like alabaster. She is about sixty.

She was dressed in a blue blouse and a long blue skirt, the uniform of the Fire Brigade Ambulance Corps. Five days ago, she told me, while cycling through London, a taxi knocked her down.

"The attack of the Panzers," Wells interjected.

I asked her whether she had driven an ambulance through the big blitz nights. "No," she replied, "only three nights a week."

Typical British understatement. At sixty, she had driven her ambulance during the black-out right up to the huge fires set by German bombs, and then, while explosive bombs weighing 500 pounds dropped all around, while fires raged, while the streets were covered with glass, debris, and firehose, she had guided her ambulance to the hospital, unloaded the wounded, and gone back to the scene of the catastrophe for more victims.

"Only three nights a week."

Her own house had been smashed by a bomb which destroyed her valuable library. In it, she lost half a novel and notes for a book on which she had been working for ten years. Since many English authors write by hand and have no carbon copies of their work, the destruction of a manuscript means doing it all over again—if possible. I asked her whether she found writing difficult now. She said it was very difficult because one didn't know about the future, either the actual future of the book—when war conditions would permit it to be printed—or the future of the world in general: would the book live?

Wells grasped Rose Macaulay and me by the arm and said, "I must separate you. Rose, we are going."

I had promised to take some friends to the theater. But on account of the black-out, theater performances begin at 5:30 and that would have interfered with my visit to Countess Boudberg's, so we went instead to the cinema. Dinner later in the Savoy Grill. Walter Kerr, able foreign correspondent of the *Herald Tribune*, and Quentin Reynolds of *Collier's* were there, and at the table next to ours sat John Dos Passos and Thornton Wilder, who that day had arrived by Clipper from New York to attend the P. E. N. Congress. But most of the diners were British, and about half of the men were in military uniform. I noticed that the women looked paler than usual. They disliked spoiling their complexions with inferior war-time cosmetics. Lipstick, I heard, had deteriorated in taste, smell, and kissability.

I asked the lady at my right whether any obloquy attaches to a young man in civilian clothes. "No," she replied. Since all able-bodied men of a certain age who are not engaged in more important war work are drafted into the armed forces, there is no stigma in wearing mufti. Besides, many soldiers, sailors, and airmen discard their uniforms when on leave. "Do your regulations allow that?" I asked a pilot in gray slacks.

"I don't know," he replied. "I haven't investigated."

Two British acquaintances came over to our table and drank coffee with us. Above the din of the dance jazz they repeated some jokes about the Home Guard and the army. "In case of invasion," the story goes, "it will be the duty of the Home Guard to hold back the enemy for three days so that the army can have time to evacuate."

When a Colonel Blimp heard that he protested and exclaimed, "No, I swear the Home Guard can hold them back longer than that."

The party had become a That-reminds-me session. Russell said, "Vic Oliver, you know, is Churchill's son-in-law and a very popular comedian. He recently performed on the BBC. He came to the microphone and started opening his mail. 'Bills, bills, more bills!' Vic declared. 'Never did one man owe so much to so many.' Then he added, 'When I traveled down here this morning, the bus was very crowded. Even the men were standing.'"

I like the British because they can laugh at themselves. They can laugh at Churchill who is deservedly adored, they can laugh at the army on which they depend for safety. No German would dare to laugh at Hitler, nor would Hitler laugh at himself.

CHURCHILL AND THE BRITISH GOVERNMENT

5. CHURCHILL AND THE BRITISH GOVERNMENT

THE BRITISH are not uncritical of Winston Churchill. Towards the end of my nine weeks in England a thought began to crystallize in my mind which startled me. I wanted to check it with persons who know more than I do. I spoke of it to a foreigner who knows the British government better than any other non-Britisher. He said, "I am beginning to think something like that myself." Still unsure of my view, I mentioned it to two members of the British Cabinet who took me out to lunch. One flared up and attacked me. The second turned to the first and said quietly, "There is something in what he says, you know."

My observations, conversations, interviews, travels, reading, and thinking in England convinced me that Winston Churchill is unmatched and irreplaceable as a leader of the people. But he is not a very good conductor of the war. In making national sentiment, and in reflecting national sentiment, he has no equal, and if only for that reason he must and will remain Prime Minister as long as the war lasts or as long as he lives in good health. As the strategist-politician directing the labors of the professional military men, Churchill likewise does a competent job. But he is bad on the production side. Time after time, men who work with him as well as unofficial Britishers volunteered the opinion in talks with me that "The Prime Minister has no mind for economics," or "Winston neglects the industrial picture," or, "W. C. loves his maps, ships, and planes so much that he gives too little thought to the economic aspect of war."

What Britain needs is a second prime minister, an industrial war lord, an economic partner for Churchill.

Winston Churchill is a political genius. He is the poet in politics, a Napoleonic Byron. He loves words and he loves action. In the modern age this is an essential but rare combination. Hitler has it. So has Roosevelt. In the House of Commons I have seen Churchill chuckle with boyish delight when members of Parliament enjoyed one of his witticisms. He works hard on his great speeches. He told officials of the BBC that one of his broadcasts took him fourteen hours to prepare. He devoted sixty hours to drafting his speech in the production debate in the House of Commons. He writes out his broadcasts like poems, with short lines and long lines, and sometimes one single word, such as But, will occupy a whole line. This method makes for variety of rhythm and emphasis.

Churchill also recognizes the paramount importance of saying the proper thing at the proper time. His radio address on June 22, 1941, was evidence of the genius of timing. Hitler had invaded Russia at dawn that day. America and England were amazed by the news and puzzled by its implications. Before the public could decide just what to think about this epochal development in eastern Europe, Churchill was on the radio, early

CHURCHILL AND BRITISH GOVERNMENT 83

Sunday afternoon, welcoming it as a windfall for Britain and her friends. Before anti-Soviet prejudices could come into play, Churchill told millions of listeners that England would help Russia and thus help herself. Never had a man molded the opinion of a world as Churchill did on that day by a stroke of timing.

Sometimes, a Churchill speech analyzes the past and present. Then it produces clarity. Sometimes, it announces action. Then it has force. "We shall fight them on beaches, landing grounds, in fields, in streets, and on the hills. We shall never surrender." That was the lion at bay. June 4, 1940, right after Dunkirk. "We shall bomb Germany by day as well as by night in ever-increasing measure, casting upon them month by month a heavier discharge of bombs." That was the eagle in attack. June 23, 1941.

It would be too much to say that Churchill enjoys the war. One has to be a barbarian for that. Hitler said to Nevile Henderson on August 23, 1939, "I am fifty years old. I prefer war now rather than when I am fifty-five or sixty." Hitler sees the war as a personal affair and decides by his own age when to plunge two billion men into a blood bath. For Churchill, at sixty-seven, the war can only be a physical strain, a personal hardship, and a world tragedy. Yet Chamberlain's appeasement undoubtedly irked and pained Churchill, whereas today, with all the heavy cost of war, he has a sense of exhilaration. He is a fighter and now he is fighting—under the handicaps bequeathed by his predecessors and the past. He is a boy and a statesman. There is something puckishly defiant about his attitude. He is rich in sheer animal energy and human buoyancy. He is a John Bulldog with a big brain—steel will plus supreme intelligence. He is articulate; the English usually are not. He is romantic; the English usually are not. Nevertheless, or perhaps therefore, the English people react to his every wink and smile and word. There is an almost musical harmony between Churchill and the nation he leads.

Churchill possesses the romance of the nineteenth century. In fact, he is all the centuries of British history wrapped into a sensitive bundle. But he lacks the managerial efficiency of the twentieth century. Churchill is not a great administrator.

The Churchill government is not so much a team as a school class. At Cabinet sessions, Teacher Churchill awes his pupils and entertains them. The members of the Cabinet listen and behave. Churchill talks much and the ministers talk little. But the Cabinet is not distinguished by smooth collaboration, dovetailing of talent, or long-range military, political, and economic planning. It is a mediocre Cabinet.

Churchill is far and away the ablest member of the government. With the possible exception of Lloyd George, who is seventy-nine, he is the greatest political figure in the country. Apart from supplying national leadership and cohesion, he co-ordinates the work of the three armed services. He is, actually, Minister of Defense with three assistant secretaries: David Margesson, Secretary of State for War; A. V. Alexander, First Lord of the Admiralty; and Sir Archibald Sinclair, Secretary of State for Air.

CHURCHILL AND BRITISH GOVERNMENT 85

This co-ordination is absent from the production field on which British military strength depends. Ernest Bevin, Laborite Minister of Labor and National Service, is constantly at loggerheads with Lord Beaverbrook, Conservative Minister of Supply. Beaverbrook is in charge of tank, gun, and general arms production, while Colonel Moore-Brabazon is in charge of aircraft production, and Alexander is in charge of ship construction. All should work smoothly with one another and with Bevin, who controls the supply of labor. They do not.

In 1940, Beaverbrook was Minister of Aircraft Production and he performed excellently, if chaotically, when the fate of England hung on the output of Hurricanes and Spitfires. As Minister of Aircraft Production, Beaverbrook was a member of the Production Executive of which Bevin is chairman. Later, Beaverbrook gave up the Ministry of Aircraft Production and became Minister of State. That automatically removed him from the Production Executive and he wrote Bevin a letter of resignation. Bevin's reply consisted of one sentence saying he was glad to receive Beaverbrook's resignation. But on the friendly collaboration between Bevin and Beaverbrook depends the functioning of Britain's munitions industries.

Bevin feels and thinks like a workingman and trade unionist. Beaverbrook is a big business man. He is one of the most striking individuals in Britain. They call him "pirate." He looks like one and sometimes acts like one. He is accessible, explosive, unexpected, and unsystematic, but he gets things done. He has "it." He can stir people to enthusiasm. He can make them forget themselves and drown themselves in work as he does. Hidden in his asthmatic chest is a dynamo always generating more energy. He makes many enemies. And he cannot work with Bevin. Officially, they have buried their differences. They are working towards a common goal. But they cannot forget their separate goals.

In the armed services, Churchill is supreme. The industrial side of the government's activity likewise needs a commander-in-chief. Instead of the two strong personalities—Bevin and Beaverbrook—there ought to be one who towers so much over all the others that he is the unquestioned leader and they his obedient subordinates. But Bevin will not knuckle under to Beaverbrook nor Beaverbrook to Bevin. Both are dynamic and headstrong.

This is the key personality problem in the British government. It runs deeper than mere personalities. The Churchill government is predominantly Conservative. If the Liberals are added to the Conservatives, it is predominantly capitalist with Labor playing a secondary role. Of the thirty-six ministers in the Cabinet, only seven are Laborites. Of the nine members of the all-important War Cabinet, which is the steering committee of the larger Cabinet, three are Laborites. Of these, Arthur Greenwood deals with post-war problems and does not supervise any department of war work. Clement Attlee is Lord Privy Seal, which involves no direct control of a ministry engaged in war activity, and only Bevin, as Minister of Labor, actually conducts an important branch of the government's war job. To re-

CHURCHILL AND BRITISH GOVERNMENT 87

move Bevin, therefore, and make Beaverbrook Minister of Munitions or Minister of Production would be a serious rebuff to Labor which it would bitterly resent, and Churchill is too wise to precipitate such a crisis. Neither will he appoint Bevin the supreme director of defense production. That would not make the private factory owners happy. Nor does Churchill himself relish the idea of Laborite Bevin as industrial dictator.

One sunny Saturday afternoon, I went out to visit David Lloyd George on his big farm at Churt in Surrey. I had seen him there in 1938, and he was good enough to ask me to come again. Apropos of the Churchill-Bevin-Beaverbrook tangle, I said to him, "Every big man is a little man."

"Not if he is a really big man," he replied.

I have noticed that the great men of our time prefer to be surrounded by subservient medium-caliber followers rather than by big men with independent views who talk back and might be potential rivals of their chief. Bevin as Minister of Production would rival Churchill in the importance of his war task. Churchill, accordingly, chooses to have four or five ministers of production. Beaverbrook is a check on Bevin and they all have to come to the Prime Minister for adjustments and instructions. They say in London, "Churchill tells the other members of his Cabinet, but he consults Bevin." He does not wish to consult Bevin too much.

The demand for a Minister of Production is very widespread. Churchill has repeatedly rejected it, but it comes up again and again. It finds support among members of all parties. During the production debate in the

House of Commons, on July 29, 1941, Sir John Wardlaw-Milne, a Conservative M.P., who is an expert on the subject, stated that Britain was still twenty-five per cent short of its maximum war output. This was a grave charge and it is the main source of the insistence on the creation of a Ministry of Production to centralize the manufacture of all military goods.

Churchill did not even try to dispute Sir John's figure or argument. He refused, however, to budge from his opposition to a Minister of Production. He said, "I have not been told who is to be this superman" who will be Minister of Production. A moment later he added, "When you have decided on the man let me know his name. I should be glad to serve under him—provided that I was satisfied that he possessed all the Napoleonic and Christian qualities required." Suppose England has no such superman. But when there is a big job to be done you take the biggest person available and let him try to rise to the needs of the situation. He may, while in office, increase in stature.

Ernest Bevin is the outstanding Labor leader in Churchill's Cabinet. He had never previously been in the government or even in Parliament. Most critics give him a high mark for his performance in House of Commons debates. He hits hard and when he has a principle to defend he never yields an inch. He often makes the impression of a charging bull. His speeches are impressive despite a Willkie-like absence of finish. He lacks tact and understanding of psychology, though he is richly endowed with vanity. The greatest deficiency in his equipment as a statesman is his scant acquaintance with international politics. In foreign affairs, he is a layman. He justifies Chamberlain's appeasement program in Spain and he was opposed to oil sanctions against Italy in 1936. He has all the disadvantages and advantages of decades of experience as a trade-union leader. His political outlook is narrow. But he has a profound devotion to the man who labors with his hands. The Tories dislike his boast that he is an "unskilled worker." A Tory M.P. had run down the dockers whose trade union Bevin built up and led throughout his adult life. Bevin, in the House of Commons, called him "a cad."

Like Herbert Morrison, former leader of the London County Council, now Secretary of State for Home Affairs and Home Security, and Sir Walter Citrine, secretary of the Trade Union Congress, Bevin is fiercely anti-Communist. The three of them have been antagonized beyond repair by Communists in their trade-union and party work. In fact, I have met as many bitter anti-Communists among Laborites as among Tories. Yet there is no love lost between Morrison and Bevin, and Bevin and Citrine have crossed swords in public, rather violently, during this war. Bevin wishes to stabilize wages. That is the government's policy. Citrine objects. Bevin, in charge of conscription, calls up skilled workingmen for service in the armed forces. Citrine says this embarrasses industry which is trying to manufacture more arms. The *Daily Herald*, organ of the Labor movement, supports Citrine in this matter against Bevin. Intolerant of such criticism, Bevin accused the *Herald* of "carrying on a nagging, miserable Quisling policy now every day of our lives." These harsh words will not be forgotten soon. Bevin's advancement in politics, therefore, would encounter opposition even in Labor ranks.

Herbert Morrison is an efficient Home Secretary. He has a keen quick mind. He is warm and inspires his co-workers to personal loyalty. London loves him and calls him 'Erbert or 'Erb. He works hard and lives simply. I went out with him once to the primitive country cottage of Ellen Wilkinson, his Parliamentary Secretary, where we spent the night. He joyfully accepted four cigarettes from her because his rations were exhausted. Morrison sees much with his one eye. He has a broad concept of world affairs and avidly uses the opportunities he now enjoys of studying the technique of modern government. He dreams of an English future in which workingmen will be happier and the poor no longer poor.

No one may be executed in Britain before Morrison initials the order.

"Just initials?" I asked in surprise.

"Yes," he replied, "the tradition of the Home Office requires my initials but not my signature."

Even after the King has refused mercy to a person condemned to death, the execution must still wait for Morrison's initials. Once, sitting in Morrison's antechamber in the Home Office, I started when I saw staring at me from the marble mantelpiece a red frame, about five by nine inches, with a white sheet of paper inside it on which, in large red letters at the top of the page, "Death Sentences" was printed. Below this terri-

CHURCHILL AND BRITISH GOVERNMENT 91

fying headline was a list of names and columns of data. I restrained my curiosity with difficulty and did not go closer. But when I was ushered into Morrison's inner office, he said to his secretary, "Show him the death sentences," and she led me to a shelf on which stood an exact copy of the frame and paper I had previously seen from afar. There were twelve names on the list, and opposite the names were the nature of the crime, the date the sentence was passed, date of the appeal, and the name of the court. A red line had been drawn through the first two names and their particulars, and in the last column opposite these two names was written "Executed" in red ink. Further down, I saw two names that were obviously German. They were spies who had parachuted from Nazi planes into the North Sea. Once in the water, they opened rubber boats, rowed to shore, and walked to railroad stations where the police arrested them. They spoke good English, had plenty of English money, and each carried a small radio sending and receiving set, concentrated food tablets, a compass, and a revolver. The other names inside the frame were British. Morrison told me that in the beginning it was difficult for him to write his initials when he knew that "H. M." was all that stood between a living human being and the hangman's rope. But he ultimately came to the conclusion that, especially in wartime, some people had to be killed by the state and the longer he delayed initialing the final order the more torture he would suffer during sleepless nights.

Morrison is the official guardian of Britain's freedoms. The right to enter and leave the country is granted by the Home Office which also supervises prisons and internment camps. Notwithstanding ample provocation by the Communists, whose propaganda before Hitler's invasion of Russia was vehemently anti-war and anti-government, only one Communist has been arrested in England since the war and that because he wrote to a minister boasting that he had directly instigated acts of sabotage in factories. Many members of the nobility and of Sir Oswald Mosley's Blackshirt Fascists, however, were interned after they openly supported Germany against their own country. When some of them created disorders in their camps a loud clamor arose in England for the withdrawal of their privileges (they are allowed to receive women visitors and buy beer which is scarce) and for their punishment. "My critics," Morrison said to me, "seem to forget that these people, for whom I hold no sympathy at all, have nevertheless not been condemned for any crime and I cannot punish them."

This is what is so attractive about the British. They refuse, in fighting Nazi Germany, to become Nazis themselves. They safeguard their liberties as zealously in wartime as in peacetime, in fact more so because the assaults on freedom are more numerous. The sanctity of the individual is protected to a surprising degree; Parliament exercises greater influence on the course of events than before the war; and the press, with the exception of the London *Daily Worker* which Morrison suppressed—the authorities close their eyes to a substitute sheet—is unfettered and only censored against the possible revelation of military secrets. When you are

CHURCHILL AND BRITISH GOVERNMENT 93

fighting a war for democracy throughout the world, the British say, you must not cripple democracy in your own country. I was passionately devoted to the Spanish Republic and did what I could to help it in its fight for freedom. It was an enlightened democracy. But there is far more political democracy in Britain now than there was in the Spanish Republic during its war in 1936-1939.

Inevitably, civil liberties are curtailed to some extent, and members of Parliament have aired grievances on the floor of the House of Commons. Often they obtain redress for aggrieved persons, including, occasionally, enemy aliens. The British treated their anti-Nazi Germans and anti-fascist Italians much more intelligently than did the France of Daladier and Bonnet, but hundreds of refugees suffered indignities and cruelties at the hands of reactionary British officials. Moreover, proved anti-fascists are denied the right to fight fascism. For instance, Arthur Koestler, whose books are widely read and highly prized in England, enlisted in the British army but was not admitted into a combatant unit and had to go into the Pioneers where, as he says, he is "digging for victory." By and large, however, Britain has safeguarded the principles of democracy and its own sanity. No small credit for this goes to Winston Churchill, who is a passionate defender of liberty at home. There he shows himself the nineteenth-century liberal. Morrison ably seconds Churchill.

If it were not for his pronounced personal characteristics, Morrison might have been elected leader of the Labor Party. Instead the choice went to Attlee.

Clement Richard Attlee is a skillful parliamentarian and irrepressible debater. Glamour, dynamics, charm, and grace are not his noticeable qualities. Nor could he be accused of radicalism. In 1940, Leopold Amery, Conservative Secretary of State for India and Burma, urged the Cabinet to introduce some progressive reforms in India. Churchill opposed the change and Attlee and Greenwood supported Churchill against Amery. The Labor leaders, in this case, may have had special motives, but I do not find that Attlee's views on India are different from those of a good many Tories.

Arthur Greenwood, Minister without portfolio, is intelligent, brave, and friendly. In the early weeks of this war, when he substituted for Attlee as Labor spokesman in the House, he delivered several brilliant speeches which have written his name permanently into the nation's history. But physical hardships and an easy-going nature militate against his influencing the course of the war. His Labor colleague, Albert Victor Alexander, the affable First Lord of the Admiralty, is a fine public speaker and looks like an old admiral though he is, in reality, an old organizer of co-operatives. He is popular with the British Navy. The last Laborite of ministerial status is Dr. Hugh Dalton, Minister of Economic Warfare or Minister of Blockade. He struggles hard with a difficult task which is romantic despite its millions of pedestrian details.

No Labor leader in the Churchill government is distinguished by stellar brilliance or earth-shaking talent. This is equally true of most other members of the present British Cabinet. Churchill is the only sun and its light hides all his ministers. When Churchill formed his government he did not say: Who are the thirty British men and women best fitted to lead the country in war? He did not say: Is David Margesson the best Secretary of State for War I can find in England? Margesson, he reasoned, had been the Chief Whip of the Conservative Party in the House of Commons and must be included in the government. Churchill could not have come to the conclusion that Sir Kingsley Wood, Chancellor of the Exchequer, is the best financial brain the country possesses. Sir Kingsley Wood is one of the big bosses of the Tory party and therefore he was selected for the post of Chancellor of the Exchequer. When the Labor Party agreed to join the Churchill Cabinet, it was part of the bargain that Clement Attlee and Arthur Greenwood should enter the War Cabinet. They are the leaders of the Labor Party. The question was never raised whether they were the best persons for the job or even the best Laborites for the job. Such procedure does not insure the most efficient conduct of the war.

"The present government has plain weaknesses in personnel, in character and in understanding," declares *The Economist*, serious, staid weekly catering to the interests of business men, bankers, and government officials. "New men in weak places," it adds, "might make a government in London worthier of England's—and the Empire's—united will to win the war." But *The Economist* is not optimistic about the prospects of getting a better government soon.

Aneurin Bevan, brilliant young member of Parliament, formerly a Welsh miner and still very Welsh in his humor, energy, and combativeness, wrote some time ago in the British left-wing Labor weekly, *The Tribune*, "Mr. Churchill, Mr. Attlee, Mr. Greenwood, Sir John Anderson, Sir Kingsley Wood, Lord Halifax, Lord Beaverbrook deceive themselves if they imagine they are the last and final expression of the British people's will to victory. If they prove inadequate they will be swept aside."

Mr. Churchill will sleep securely, in the afternoon too as is his wont, despite this attack. For even Aneurin Bevan, I suspect, would not vote to expel Churchill from No. 10 Downing Street because any successor who is politically possible would, from Bevan's viewpoint too, be much worse. He would gladly oust the old appeasers still in and near the Cabinet: Halifax, (Sir John) Simon, now Viscount and Lord Chancellor, Sir Samuel Hoare, ambassador in Madrid, and others. Churchill, however, is there to stay.

The British discuss Churchill's successor only in connection with ill health, of which there is happily no sign, or of his regretted death from natural causes or through bombing. The man I heard mentioned most often as next Prime Minister is Foreign Secretary Robert Anthony Eden, Conservative, born June 12, 1897. Some persons suggest Bevin, others mention Beaverbrook or Sir John Anderson, now Lord President of the Council. An organization called Mass Observation conducted a poll on this subject and announced that Sir Stafford Cripps received quite a number of votes as the Prime Minister to come after Churchill. (The very fact of such a poll is striking; it would, of course, have been impossible in Germany, Spain, Russia, Italy, or Japan.) Cripps, born in 1889, was ambassador to the Soviet government at the beginning of the Russo-German war and his prestige has risen enormously. He is one of England's three best lawyers. The Labor Party expelled him in 1939 because he was too left-wing and too pro-Communist. Since then he has lived in Russia and has presumably altered his views on revolution and socialism. By family, wealth, schooling, and professional standing, Cripps is of those who traditionally rule Britain. (His father was Lord Parmoor.) His integrity is universally known and recognized. He is puritanical and ascetic; he lives on raw fruits and vegetables. He is a crusader for exalted causes, has a passion for social justice, and gets a wide hearing in the House of Commons and in the country. He may play an important political role in England. His relations with Churchill are based on mutual respect and understanding. But he is not nearly as popular as Anthony Eden.

Eden had many followers, and "fans," among Conservatives, Liberals, and Laborites. He is usually remembered as an anti-appeaser and an opponent of Neville Chamberlain, not so much because of Loyalist Spain as because of Abyssinia, Austria, and Italy. He has glamour, intelligence, smiles nicely, makes a good appearance, and speaks with pleasant forcefulness in public.

England would like an Eden as Prime Minister. His friends say he is weak. But that could only enhance his chances; Sir Kingsley Wood, the Conservative Party boss, might hope to dominate him, Sir John Anderson might hope to be the power behind an Eden throne, and Labor would not fear him.

For administrative ability, the Cabinet has no equal to Sir John Anderson. He is a strong man with a strong face who has gone through hard experiences as governor in Ireland and India. His mind functions like a filing cabinet; everything in it is neatly catalogued with cross references, and after a hundred minutes with him a crystal-clear picture of the general situation will emerge. He is Churchill's bottleneck breaker and man-for-all-emergencies. When Churchill sailed across the Atlantic in the summer of 1941 to meet President Roosevelt, he instructed Anderson to prepare the occupation of Persia. It involved the British Army, the British Navy, supplies, propaganda, relations with India, relations with Persia, and relations with Russia. This was Sir John's specialty: a job requiring a vast amount of coordination. He is the cold, dispassionate civil servant elevated to a high post in politics. Government for him is first of all a technique of management. It is a mechanism. He made the impression on me of a tank. Given a task, he grinds through obstacles by sheer weight, power, and forward drive. A tank, not an aeroplane. He does not fly.

I said to someone who knows him well, "He really thinks."

"Yes," was the reply. "But he has no imagination. The lines on his face are those of a thinker, but he has none of the Lincoln lines of human sympathy. I should

CHURCHILL AND BRITISH GOVERNMENT 99

hate to see him Prime Minister of Britain after the war. He could be cruel."

One subject lifts Sir John Anderson out of his mathematical reserve: India. In talking about it he reveals a nostalgia unbefitting a tank. I also discussed India with the Right Honorable Leopold Charles Maurice Stennett Amery, Secretary of State for India and for Burma. He is a remarkable character, gentle, human, and complicated.

I interviewed Amery off the record for an hour and a half in the dismal old India Office and afterwards he invited me to have dinner informally with him and his family. When I arrived at his home he had just returned from a conference of the Inter-Allied governments which he attended as one of Britain's three delegates. Opposite him, at the table, had sat Ivan Maisky, the Soviet ambassador. The newspapers that day were reporting the valiant resistance of the Russians around Moscow. Amery had taken paper and pencil and written in Russian a verse from a famous Russian poem about the battle against Napoleon at Borodino. He passed the note to Maisky. Maisky answered in Russian, expressing surprise at Amery's knowledge of the Russian language, and then added a compliment in English. Amery took Maisky's note from his pocket, showed it to me, and then went on quoting from the poem. We exchanged some sentences in Russian. Amery has never been to Russia. During this war, he has been broadcasting in Turkish from London to Turkey. He also speaks Greek, Serbian, Bulgarian, French, and German.

He was born in India and has probably also mastered some Indian dialects.

Amery has a small body; his feet hang down to a stool when he sits in the ornamental chair at his office desk. He has a round head and an apple face with red cheeks. He is a fighter and an unorthodox critic of the government. Though a Conservative, he consistently opposed Chamberlain's appeasement policy and inspired some of Eden's public attacks on it. He sits in Parliament for Birmingham. So did Neville Chamberlain. There are four electoral constituencies in Birmingham, Mrs. Amery explained, and Chamberlain's was the business-residential section whereas her husband's is the slums. Amery is the outstanding champion of supplementary allowances to poor families with many children. He advocates a "special provision on a national scale" whereby the state and the employers will make an "additional payment" to workingmen "in accordance with family needs." This, he says, would "correct the anti-social consequences of the individualist wage system on family life." A proposal to enact such a measure has been signed by two hundred members of Parliament, most of them Laborites.

Mrs. Amery said, "Leo represents working class voters in Parliament but he is a Conservative because he loves the Empire." Amery enjoys art and nature and has a sense of romance. Speaking of a contemplated grand Libyan offensive, he said, "There was once a Moslem conqueror—I think his name was Akbar—who swept across Northern Africa until he reached the Atlantic where he rode his horse into the sea and, holding a sword aloft in one hand and the Koran in another, called Allah to witness that he could go no further. We should like to do that too."

India is Amery's chief concern.

The British recognize that India's proximity to Burma, China, Singapore, and the Pacific stimulates the curiosity of Americans in the great Indian continent with its three hundred and fifty million inhabitants. Moreover, India's progress towards independence and freedom naturally strikes a sympathetic chord in the United States. The fate of the British empire and that of America are now so inextricably linked that no American's interests in the key problem of the British empire comes as a surprise to the intelligent Englishman. I found official and unofficial Britishers eager to share with me their views and information on India.

Even a journal like the London *New Statesman and Nation*, which calls itself socialist and has always championed the victims of imperialism, does not expect India to obtain her freedom during this war: "We do not suggest, and never have suggested, a formal constitutional change in wartime." It merely wants the British Viceroy's Council of limited powers converted into an Indian national Cabinet which will prepare for self-determination when hostilities cease.

But the end of the war will not remove what British Conservatives regard as the chief objection to Indian independence. Britishers in high position have told me that England does not wish to keep India. "We do not want India," one of them said. "We went there for selfish motives of profit. But we do not want it now for that motive or any motive. If we left India, however, the land would flow with blood from the Northwest Frontier to the southern tip of the Continent." Should Britain withdraw her armed forces and restraining influence, the argument goes, the Moslems, the wild Afridi tribes, and the Afghans would slaughter the Hindus. The Hindus are the majority in India but the Moslems—variously estimated as between seventy-five and ninety million strong—are the warlike element of the population. Now this fear, if real, would remain after the war. It would, indeed constitute a permanent barrier to Indian national independence.

How, then, can India ever become free? I posed this question to several responsible officials and received no answer. The British government has no solution of the problem of India. At best, it means to improve conditions through moderate administrative reforms and, after that, hope for the best.

I ventured to discuss this dilemma with four members of the Churchill Cabinet on four separate occasions. I said, "You say you want to get out of India but cannot. Any plan you propose for the future arouses prejudice in one section or another of India because it is a British plan. Why not allow a non-official American of Supreme Court caliber to go to India, meet the spokesmen of all classes, castes, regions, and religions, and ask them what they themselves would like to see happen to India? Maybe he, with their aid, could evolve a scheme for the solution of the Indian problem."

One member of the War Cabinet replied, "I wonder

CHURCHILL AND BRITISH GOVERNMENT 103

how the Prime Minister would react to that suggestion." He uttered these words in a hopeful tone. Another member of the War Cabinet said he would consult a colleague who knew India. A third member of the War Cabinet, a Laborite, doubted the wisdom of the proposal. One minister said, "That's an important idea."

(In the United States, I subsequently broached the idea to two members of the Supreme Court. They said, "There is everything to be said for it," and "It could certainly do no harm.")

Jawaharlal Nehru, next to Gandhi the foremost Hindu figure, contends that the differences between Hindus and Moslems are surmountable. He says, "The Moslems are a majority in five northern provinces. Under provincial autonomy they can control these five provinces." He charges that the British "encourage disruptive tendencies" between Hindus and Moslems and, as a result, bloody Hindu-Moslem battles have occurred.

The Indian nationalist, accordingly, insists that until the British get out there will be no Indian unity. A facetious Englishman, long a top-rank civil servant, pointed out that the Indians had served as "sepoys" or mercenaries for the British during many decades. "Perhaps now, the British could be the sepoys of an Indian government and keep the peace."

Churchill has no ear for such discussions of India's future. The Moslem minority and the Sikhs, who are not Hindu, supplied England with over a million soldiers in the first world war and have already poured almost a million volunteers into the British armed forces in the present conflict. That to Churchill is a paramount consideration. For the rest, the situation is not pressing, in the opinion of many Britishers, and can wait the outcome of the war.

"I could outline the Irish problem on one sheet of paper," said a British official. "But India is fifteen Irelands." It is a most intricate complex of problems. And no sudden solution may be possible. India is as complicated as Europe and not dissimilarly complicated, for both are continents inhabited by numerous races and nations that must live together. Where is the British genius that will help give Europe an intelligent peace after this war? India is a test. And India, Indian nationalists declare, is also a test of the sincerity of British avowals of an intention to make the world better and more democratic.

The Churchill-Roosevelt Atlantic Charter promised "to respect the right of all peoples to choose the form of government under which they live." Does that include us? Indians asked. No, replied Churchill in the House of Commons.

In talking with British Cabinet ministers about India I ventured to urge the release of Jawaharlal Nehru and other Indian nationalists from prison. They gave me every reason for not doing it. Then they did it. Imagination, daring, and a healthy disregard for legalistic red tape can accomplish great results. But imagination and daring are what the Cabinet lack. It is a government with a defensive psychology and normally shies away from enterprise.

"Why has Churchill no spirit of adventure?" I asked Lloyd George.

CHURCHILL AND BRITISH GOVERNMENT 105

"His sense for adventure was broken by his great misadventure in the last war—Gallipoli," Lloyd George replied.

Whether it be Churchill's mental pattern or Britain's military and economic weakness, the fact is that the British government has usually waited until the enemy forced its hand. The initiative has generally been Hitler's or Japan's.

I talked with Lord Woolton, Minister of Food, a well-meaning humanitarian whose labor policy in his own department stores has always been enlightened. Now too he rarely makes an important move without consulting the trade unions. He has handled the food situation extremely well. Almost everyone in Britain receives enough nourishment, in some cases more than before the war, even though the diet is monotonous and even though the rich can get more than the poor. I heard few grumblings about food. "Not so bad, you know," workers said to me in factories in Yorkshire when I asked about their food. But the proof of the abnormality of the food situation is that food has become a common topic of conversation. The less food the more talk about it. Of the food jokes, one was so good that I cabled it to the New York *Nation*. Vivien Leigh, famous film star, is in England and she received a letter from a friend in America asking whether she wanted any food sent her. Now the British censorship does not allow such questions to be answered in the affirmative, so Miss Leigh replied, "No, but send me a bad actor." I took my dispatch to the censor one Sunday evening. He read it and passed it, but he must have thought this a strange American idea of what's funny, for not one Englishman in fifty—I afterwards tried it—knows that a bad actor is a "ham."

Lord Woolton, Minister of Food, has an able assistant in the genial Major Gwilym Lloyd George, son of the ex-Prime Minister. At dinner in his hotel once, there were the major, his wife, an RAF squadron commander, and I. The major and the commander did not take sugar with their coffee and Mrs. Lloyd George and I, overjoyed, appropriated the two half-lumps which the waiter had served them. Mrs. Lloyd George said that is what she missed most: sugar. It is a matter of shipping. There is plenty of sugar in the world but not enough ships to carry adequate quantities to Britain. Most English people told me that the country needed concentrated fruit juices, powdered milk, and vitamins from America, in addition to what they were already getting under the Lease-Lend Act. They were clearly grateful for everything America was sending.

Sir Archibald Sinclair, Secretary of State for Air, had a different request from the United States: more and bigger bombers. He regards the giant bomber as the key to victory over Germany. He has charm and political insight, and he, the Liberal, fought Chamberlain's disastrous appeasement policy as passionately as Churchill or any of the Laborites. Indeed, he was more consistent than Churchill and than some Laborites in that he immediately and passionately supported Loyalist Spain where this second world war was born.

Viscount Cranborne, Secretary for Dominion Affairs, understood the British stake in Spain too, and he would

CHURCHILL AND BRITISH GOVERNMENT 107

have gone to war to defeat Franco and the Italo-German invasion of Spain. I was having lunch with him and two other Conservative ministers when he said this. His two colleagues in the government demurred, one mildly, the other completely. Cranborne belongs to the ancient Cecil family and is, I was told, a descendant of Queen Elizabeth. He nevertheless has advanced ideas on social changes after the war. He knows that the old Elizabethan and Victorian England is dying. And since he doesn't wish England to die he wants a new England to be born. Many of his fellow-Conservatives think as he does on this matter. They are the younger Conservatives.

A rising star among them is Brendan Bracken, Minister of Information and a newspaper owner. He has red hair but isn't bound by red tape. His decision are quick and unhampered by little principles. He was Churchill's private and trusted secretary, and in that capacity he built up an intimacy with the P.M. which is a great asset.

Even the young Conservatives do not go very far in their social thinking, and Churchill does not go along with them. Churchill sees the war chiefly as a military struggle and devotes himself to that aspect of the fight to the exclusion of the social changes which must be undertaken or promised and sketched so that the nation may actually see a new life taking shape. It is Hitler's New Order or a New Democratic Order. But the old order of Chamberlain, Lord Simon (who is still in the government despite his surrender to Japan in China in 1932), Sir Montagu Norman, Lord Londonderry, Sir

Samuel Hoare, and the whole Conservative party is struggling fiercely to maintain its hold on the country. And, says *The Economist*, "It is not Mr. Churchill that has captured the Conservative machine; it would appear to be the Conservative machine that has captured Mr. Churchill."

The position is simple: the British people have seen their rulers, blind, cowardly, and inept, get them into a war by a series of abject surrenders to Japan, Mussolini, Hitler, and Franco. The country arrived at the brink of disaster wholly unprepared. That was the fault of the men who led the country. For they had plenty of warning of the intentions of the fascist aggressors. The average British citizen, therefore, does not want to be ruled after the war by the same sort of people who ruled him, or rather misruled him, before the war. Yet he sees those very people, organized as the Conservative party, retrenching their power behind the broad back of Winston Churchill without whom they would have been swept into the dustbin of history. The British nation is being told not to worry about what is coming after the war. "First things first. First let us win the war." But it is the Conservatives who are worrying about what will happen afterwards, and they are preparing against it with a zeal which would have been commendable if it had been lavished on preparations against Hitler before September 3, 1939.

How does this interfere with the energetic prosecution of the war?

WHITHER ENGLAND?

6. WHITHER ENGLAND?

IT is an undeniable fact that the vast majority of the leaders in every walk of life in this country are drawn from a class which includes barely one-twentieth of the population." This quotation is from the sober, respectable London *Economist*. These leaders, *The Economist* proceeds, are "not selected on the basis of ability."

The Economist has put its finger unerringly on the spot of Britain's vital illness. "The United Kingdom, with a population of 48 million inhabitants," it declares, "is being run by such brains as can be found in a population of two millions plus the few exceptional individuals who crash the barrier." The barrier is wealth and social position. Britain is ruled by those fortunate enough to be born in the right kind of family. "This cannot be an efficient use of the native talent of the country," *The Economist* concludes.

"We are very short of talent," I heard over and over again in England. The explanation usually given was Britain's heavy casualties in the first world war. "The gifted men who would be running England now, the men between forty and fifty, are buried in Flanders and France," people said. That sounds plausible. But it is only the most obvious reason; it is not the most important reason.

Germany and Russia also suffered heavy casualties

during the first world war. Yet they had no scarcity of capable leaders in most walks of life. The German republic, and then the Nazis, as well as the Bolsheviks, tapped new sources of talent. New strata of society gave their sons and daughters to manage those countries. Their ideas and methods may be obnoxious; they nevertheless possessed initiative, drive, and the will to do and to govern. But England, after 1918, relied on the same classes as before 1914. And in those classes the deaths and wounds of the war did, of course, take a terrible toll. For that very reason, 1918 should have been followed by social changes which would have given new groups access to leadership. This was not the case. The brains of the two million have not done badly considering the limited supply available. But the other forty-six million have rich stores of intelligence and are offering them to the nation. That is the real revolution knocking at Britain's door.

For England, To Be or Not To Be means whether it is to be run by the two or the forty-eight. Will British democracy, in other words, become more democratic? Britain has simply lacked enough leaders with vitality, ability, and adaptability. Winston Churchill is an exception. There are others. But these few do not alter the general fact. The poverty of talent is encountered not only in politics, though it is found chiefly in politics and particularly in national politics which has been the monopoly of a narrow British oligarchy. The emergence of Labor as a significant factor in national life brought a change, but the change was slight because Labor did not wield much power and had its own

WHITHER ENGLAND?

caste system. Among Conservatives, a place in politics is usually the reward for having chosen the right father, preferably one with a title, or for having made a fortune in business. Among Laborites, there is a premium on length of undistinguished service, on colorless subservience to the higher-ups, and on orthodoxy.

In many fields of activity, old age itself has been considered an asset and youth an embarrassment. A general, it seems, had to be old; the Bank of England recently waived a strict though unwritten rule in order to allow Sir Montagu Norman to remain its head after he had passed the retirement age of seventy. "Even *The Economist* objects to his reappointment," comments the *New Statesman and Nation*, which calls Norman "that ancient and remarkable autocrat," "dictator," and "symbol of a financial orthodoxy which has been utterly disastrous for England and for the world."

The British people are losing faith in the type of person that has traditionally ruled England. In 1918, Great Britain won a great victory. Then British statesmen threw away the victory and led the country down the path of surrender to the second world war. The nation wondered why England, a major power, had become so weak. Something happened as the nation wondered. The nation decided that its leaders were at fault. The blunders of Stanley Baldwin, the blunders of Neville Chamberlain, the blunders of appeasement, have opened many eyes.

B. L. Combes is a plain British coal miner. *Picture Post* is a large-circulation London weekly whose god is J. B. Priestley. The *Picture Post* prints an article by

Combes. He writes about the opened eyes: "Those blunders have finished forever the tradition of a class that was born to govern." The "divine right" of a certain set of Englishmen to rule England has been shattered. They know it. They are bracing to meet the storm.

On June 11, 1941, Foreign Secretary Anthony Eden announced in the House of Commons that the British diplomatic service would be opened to men and women "without private means." For centuries, the diplomatic service has been the reserved occupation of a small class of well-to-do graduates of "public schools," who wear the "old school tie" of Eton, Harrow, and so forth. They wear striped trousers and cutaways beautifully. But they made a mess of British diplomacy. They carry umbrellas. Mr. Combes, the miner, says, "We want more sledge-hammer users in our government and fewer umbrella carriers." The umbrella carriers cultivate the famous Oxford accent or even the Cambridge accent, but few can speak to the hearts of the peoples at whose capitals they represent His Majesty's Government.

Nothing in that closed diplomatic world has changed as a result of the second world war. But the need of a change has been recognized.

Politics likewise suspects that a new day is dawning. British politics is free from the ordinary forms of corruption. Ugly graft is unknown. But the Conservative Party, which is the majority party, admits that seats in Parliament are for sale. Parliament selects the Prime Minister and his government. Parliament alone can overthrow the government. It is therefore extremely important who sits in Parliament. Yet money may unlock the door to membership in Parliament.

The Central Council of the National Union of Conservative and Unionist Associations, key body of the Conservative Party, held a meeting in Caxton Hall, London, on October 2, 1941, which aired the question of the sale of parliamentary seats. It adopted a resolution deploring the "unreasonable financial conditions [which] debar suitable candidates from consideration." Sir Derrick Gunston, Conservative member of Parliament, who moved the resolution, explained that "in certain constituencies suitable candidates cannot even be considered"—because a rich man has already bought the nomination. He buys the nomination in a safe district where nomination is as good as election. "What a picture for the future," Sir Derrick exclaimed, "when so much depends on the successful working of almost the last remaining democracy." What a picture indeed! "A promise of a large contribution," Sir Derrick continued, "has far too often been the determining factor in the selection of a candidate." He went on, significantly: "It is some of these financial agreements which are the main cause of keeping out the right type of candidate. These unhealthy customs do immense harm to an ancient and honorable party." They do.

In a mood of confession, Mrs. Tait, Conservative M.P., told the meeting that her election had cost her eleven hundred pounds, a large sum in England, which she had contributed to the party. Further, in accordance with an arrangement, she paid the party the whole of her parliamentary salary—four hundred pounds a year—

(it has since been raised to six hundred) for the first three years after election and also gave subscriptions to various funds. Major Maxwell Fyfe, who supported the motion, called these subscriptions by candidates a form of "whitemail."

As a result of such practices, British politics is full of expensive dead wood. After this war started, Captain Ramsay, Conservative M.P. for the constituency of Peebles, was arrested for treason. He is still in prison. *The Economist* prints his biography and then says editorially. "He is M.P. for Peebles because he comes of the right sort of family, because he married a daughter of the peerage and the widow of a very rich man, because he went to the right school and joined the right regiment. If his father had been a bank clerk and his wife the daughter of an insurance agent, if he had been educated in a local school, gone with a scholarship to Oxford [if he had been poor and studious, in other words] and made his way on his own brains to a moderate competence in a respectable trade or profession, then he might have bombarded every political association on the books of the [Conservative] Central Office for a constituency, and every time the odds against his getting into the House of Commons would have been a thousand to one."

This situation, *The Economist* declares, has had disastrous effects on recent British history. Captain Ramsay, it says, was one of many. "These tenth-rate nonentities who have been jobbed into the House of Commons because they were men of the 'right type' provided just the background that the Government required for its calamitous foreign policy and for its blindness to the danger in which the country stood. The government needed behind it a solid block of M.P.'s stupid enough to jeer at Mr. Churchill, to admire the moral grandeur of Stanley Baldwin and to applaud the foresight of Mr. Chamberlain." There is, the paper warns, "a long score to settle with the men who put Captain Ramsay and his like into Parliament."

The root of this evil runs deep. The British nation has not been as well-educated, as well-fed, as well-housed, and as well-clothed as a rich, advanced country like Britain could afford to be. The schools available in normal times to the common people of Britain have much poorer facilities than those which the "public schools" offer to the privileged few. Moreover, the school-leaving age everywhere is very low. In 1941, the London municipality fixed a school-leaving age of 16 as a goal to be attained seven years after the end of the war. The distinction in living standards and educational opportunities between the thin upper crust in Britain and the broad mass of the people is extremely sharp. The war has thrown a bright spotlight on this distinction. The man who drops his h's has become conscious of it. He has seen the disastrous mistakes of his "superiors." He has also, under Hitler's bombs, recognized the good qualities of his own kind of folk. This started the assault on the privileged castes of England.

Some contend that it is not necessary to worry, that after the war the rich will be too poor to support the expensive public schools, and that the result will be social leveling. Some contend that this is not the time to insist on breaking up the social strata, that all attention ought to be concentrated on the defeat of Hitler. The answer they receive is that even today the two million privileged still seek to bar the other forty-six million from positions of leadership and trust; they thus obstruct the successful prosecution of the war.

The two million are tenacious and resourceful. They enjoy many strategic and tactical advantages in this silent second war that proceeds parallel with the war against the Fascist International. But occasionally, the forty-six million win a skirmish. The Conservative Party acknowledges that it needs brains as well as gold; Mr. Eden realizes that the diplomatic service needs new blood as well as blue bloods; even the army is feeling a fresh wind. Some younger generals—one aged forty-five—have been appointed. Early in 1941, Lieutenant Colonel R. C. Bingham, commander of an officers' training academy of the British army wrote a letter to the London *Times* complaining that the new officers from the working class and the lower middle class, unadorned by the "old school tie," had fallen down on the job. "Never was an old school tie, and the best it stands for, more justified than today," he wrote. Colonel Bingham himself wears the tie of Eton. But he is no longer in charge of that officers' training academy. Secretary of State for War Margesson, yielding to a storm of protest, announced in the House of Commons that "this officer is no longer suitable for command of an officers' training unit."

To be sure, Colonel Bingham was not the only Colonel Blimp in the British army, and the many who remain still hope to blimp their way to victory. But a struggle is on to make the army more democratic and less blimpish. Joseph C. Harsch's *Pattern of Conquest*, a good book on Nazi Germany, points out that among the important reasons for the German army's triumphs in this war is that "in it caste is dead and merit has taken its place." The British know this, but old traditions die hard and those who benefit by them fight for their perpetuation. The RAF is young and has no rusty traditions. Its chiefs are young. The garage mechanic is likely to fly better than the boy trained to look smart in an Eton collar. No one shouts commands in the RAF as they do in the British army. There is no premium, therefore, on the voice and demeanor of synthetic superiority which have long been regarded as assets in British army officers.

The reverses of the British army in this war, and the successes of the German army, have shaken the British military out of their lethargy and complacency. The fine work of the RAF and the navy has goaded them into introducing some mild reforms. Indeed, a few of these were launched before the war started. When Leslie Hore-Belisha was Secretary of State for War he ruled, for instance, that all officers must come up through the ranks before receiving their commissions. This regulation tended to break down the snobbery of those who, because of birth or wealth, could step out of a tuxedo into a captain's uniform. Occasionally the press reports infringements of the Hore-Belisha innovation. But the trend is in the healthy direction. Soldiers and non-commissioned officers who have distinguished themselves in active service are given priority for admission to officers' training units and win quicker promotion. (This is likewise true of several English friends of mine whose military experience was gained in the Spanish Loyalist army.)

"Of course," one soldier writes to a British publication, "there is unfairness in the fact that the man with a good education stands a better chance of being chosen to attend an officers' cadet school than the man with a poor education. This means an advantage to the rich and well-to-do. But the blame rests with the social system, not with the army."

Leslie Hore-Belisha's reforms won him supreme unpopularity among the old-type blimp officers, who finally got his scalp when he made some mistakes of policy which displeased Churchill. The Colonel Blimps of old England continue the struggle against the new England. When the British army went to France in 1939, officers and men wore the same uniform; that strengthened the democratic spirit. Since then the officers have won advantages for themselves in dress, vacations, and general living conditions. The soldiers accordingly complain that the further an officer is from danger the better the army command treats him. Besides, family and money still count. But they count for less. Political convictions are no bar to useful national service. Ex-Communists are trusted in the armed forces if they deserve to be trusted. Socialists, here and there, suffer discrimination, but those cases are exceptions. The British are a tolerant race. Tolerance makes for greater loyalty and democracy.

Class prejudices and class barriers have not been obliterated in Britain. They are, however, under constant bombardment. War means death, and death is the great equalizer. Then why not equality in the face of death? Sir Richard Acland, a well-to-do Liberal member of Parliament, made a speech some time ago which began, "I am appealing to my fellow members of the privileged classes of this country." He appealed to the rich to pay their taxes cheerfully because, he calculated, even after a supertaxpayer had met all his obligations to the Treasury he still earned as much as fifty Spitfire pilots combined. "Let us see the man," Sir Richard challenged, "who claims that his contribution to the war effort is equal to that of fifty Spitfire pilots." But Acland did not stop there. He appealed to his fellow-privileged to give up more than money. "I am appealing to them," he said, "to maintain national unity by giving up something much more important: their personal power over the economic life of this country." There he is demanding a very great sacrifice.

The strain of war has revealed all the cracks and weaknesses of the economic system of England and showed how backward British business has been during the last two decades. Until this war, Britain, under Conservative leadership, was slipping.

Between 1919 and 1923, Germany lived through a period of extreme currency inflation. The Germans used cheap money to build new industries. In 1924, the Dawes Plan was introduced as a method of collecting war reparations from Germany. Billions of dollars consequently flowed into the country in the form of foreign loans. These funds financed more German industrial construction. That lasted until 1929. Germany was a prosperous country. In 1933, the Nazis arrived with their dynamic of rearmament, and they erected new manufacturing plants—so that, when this war commenced, Germany, as a production machine, was new and up-to-date. That explains most of Hitler's victories on the field of battle.

Under her several Five-Year Plans, Soviet Russia likewise inaugurated gigantic schemes of industrial renovation and expansion. For Russia, this war came twenty-five years too soon. A generation from now Russia would have completed the task of industrialization, and her people, who graduated only recently from the era of wood into the epoch of steel and concrete, would have mastered modern industrial technique. Then Russia would have been more than a match for any fighting nation.

Great Britain's business men, however, did not possess the wisdom, the will, and the energy to scrap the old and build anew. England was the first country to change from handicraft to machine industry. Since that industrial revolution, however, England has allowed younger nations to overtake and pass her. Why this lack of initiative? Was it the stick-in-the-mud attitude of Sir Richard Acland's privileged friends? I was inspecting a munitions plant in Yorkshire, and the managing director introduced me to two engineers in one department who visited America in 1937. In a Cleveland plant, they had noticed a superior method of handling material, and they endeavored, when they returned home, to have it adopted by the management. The management resisted for two years and yielded only after the war broke out. "Remember?" one of the engineers asked the managing director.

"I do, indeed," the director replied.

Was England an old tired country without the resources to vie with Germany, America, Russia, and Japan? Or did her industrial leaders lack faith in England and prefer to invest their wealth abroad and in the empire? The fact is that England did not modernize her industry. She also failed to encourage the industrialization of her dominions and colonies. That accounts for Britain's weakness in this war. Napoleon once said that armies march on their bellies; they depended for progress on the food they could find. Nowadays, armies fight on their factories. This is a tank and aeroplane war. The first world war required five men behind the lines to supply each soldier at the front with his arms, food, and clothing. Today, it is not five but sixteen. War has become more motorized and mechanized. So has Germany become more motorized and mechanized. England has not kept pace.

I have always been amused, on my frequent trips to England in peacetime, by the tiny wooden railway freight cars for transporting coal. Each had painted on it the name of C. W. Stewart or R. F. Forster or Gibbert & Sloan, and so forth. The man who owns the coal mine also owns the freight car. He used to fill the freight car with coal, send it several hundred miles if necessary to his customer, and then have it shunted back again to his mine. Since the war this system has been abandoned. A coal freight car now moves from the mine to the nearest customer and then to the nearest mine. All coal cars have been pooled. Some such arrangement was needed a century ago. It required the compulsion of war to make the British drop this glaringly inefficient method.

In my fourteen years in Russia, I visited hundreds of newly built factories. The director usually greeted his visitor with a little speech, "This is the most modern plant in Europe. Actually, we started working only the day before yesterday, and six months ago wheat still grew where we are now standing."

More recently, I went through some factories in the north of England. The director, supremely cordial, would say, "Would you like first to see our archeological museum? You know, we date back to Roman times." Sometimes the factory showed it.

In part, to be sure, this is a caricature. The Romans, according to report, did not use aeroplanes, and Britain's new aviation industry supplies the RAF with the finest machines in the world. In the last decade, many up-to-date factories have been built in England. Great housing projects were carried out. But Britain's railroads, mines, steel mills, textile industry, gas and lighting systems, and housing needed thorough renovation after the first world war and did not get it. The privileged moneyed classes made the stability of money a fetish to which they sacrificed industrial growth. Industrial backwardness and obsolescence are the chief explanation of Britain's lack of offensive military power.

Economic self-sufficiency was the goal inspired by the

first world war. This yearning for national industrial independence found expression in the Bolshevik revolution, in the ferment in China and India, and in fascism. Normally, nations undergoing industrialization need more imports. But high tariff barriers, social and political unrest, international suspicion and prejudice, and the policy of fascism to close open trade doors reduced the volume of world commerce on which England's prosperity depends so much. Moreover, the United States had become the center of the world's financial and industrial power, and Japan, Germany, and even Italy were invading traditionally British overseas markets. Britain was hard hit. But instead of rousing herself to a supreme effort and reasserting the might she had in her she was lulled to sleep by the complacent Stanley Baldwin and the defeatist Neville Chamberlain who led the country from 1931 to 1941. Just when England needed leaders of genius it fell into the hands of her most mediocre politicians. Was this a tragic accident? Or does a ruling class which is incapable of great deeds naturally gravitate towards incapable leaders? Churchill was always there. But they wouldn't have him. "He's too brilliant," they said. That meant he might have attempted to stir them out of their sloth and in doing so reveal their impotence. The British ruling class hoped to prolong its life by being passive when nobody disturbed it or by retreating when someone did disturb it. When Hitler, Japan, and Mussolini caused disturbances, it retreated; that was appeasement. The Baldwins, Chamberlains, Simons, and Hoares trusted to luck or chance or a miracle that would turn these obstreperous totalitarian upstarts away from them or tame them or destroy them. They trusted and waited and thereby gave heart to the aggressors and thereby brought on the second world war. Now the class which had hoped to save itself by doing nothing is called upon to save England in a war which demands more energy, initiative, and strength than any conflict in human history. The British people feel that a class whose finest flower was Baldwin and Chamberlain cannot cope with this gigantic task. But the instinct of self-preservation is still powerful among the privileged groups of Great Britain and they refuse to relinquish their monopoly of leadership. Their purpose is to win the war without losing their economic advantages which Sir Richard Acland asks them to relinquish. They realize that war, which concentrates authority in the government and fills the common folk with a feeling of their own importance, is a threat to those advantages. That is another reason why Chamberlain sought, at all costs, to avoid war. But now the war is there and it has stirred up considerable disrespect, distrust, and dislike of the old class of rulers.

War overtook an unprepared Britain. Victorious in the last war, the nation became pacifist. But the government could always have aroused the people to the dangers of unpreparedness. It never tried. Actually, the people and some of its leaders had to arouse the government. How could Chamberlain have fostered rearmament when he did not think Hitler, Japan, and Mussolini were a menace? He came back from Munich in September, 1939, waving that miserable scrap of paper which he had signed with Hitler and exclaiming, "It is peace for our time." If it was peace for our time, why arm? As late as 1939, Chamberlain was resisting popular pressure for an all-out defense program. A lady said to me recently, "Chamberlain was asleep at the switch." That is paying him too high a compliment. He was asleep, but nowhere near the switch.

When the war broke out, therefore, Britain endeavored desperately to regain lost time. While I was in England, numerous new munitions plants whose foundations were laid on the very eve of the war or, in most cases, after the commencement of the war, were just beginning to turn out arms. The nation willingly girded itself for maximum effort. It reduced its consumption of food and goods to a minimum. Nevertheless, the country had not yet reached the peak of industrial output or of national effort.

Complaints were heard about the slowness with which the military authorities placed contracts for arms and about the inexperience of civil servants and government ministers who were supervising industry's work for the state. There were complaints, too, against manufacturers. Neither manufacturers nor officials, however, criticized workingmen. Occasionally, to be sure, the charge of absenteeism was made against workers. But the government's Select Committee on National Expenditure, investigating industrial conditions, recommended that "Workpeople should have one day's rest in seven." Wherever this is not the case, some hands absent themselves. This does not alter the fact that British Labor's behavior and loyalty to country have been exemplary. Strikes are not prohibited by law. Few last more than a day or two at the most. Only rarely does a strike involve the basic principle of the right to organize in trade unions; this is universally conceded in Britain. The majority of the strikes result from demands for higher pay or objection to reduced pay. The average number of workingmen on strike in defense industries as well as other industries, in any month in 1941 was 30,000. Labor has put its shoulder stoutly to the wheel in order to save the country in which it has achieved so many rights and advantages. Labor feels that this is its war. It knows what has happened to Labor in fascist and fascist-occupied lands. Workingmen throughout Britain, accordingly, do not mutter when hard-won trade-union privileges are whittled down or when additional sacrifices or duties are imposed upon them. Labor's big grievance is that it is not permitted to do more.

In several factories which I visited workingmen pointed out to me how they could increase output. They said they knew their machines and shops as well as the management, and because they all had an interest in winning the war they ought to collaborate in running the factory. The Trade Union Congress of 1941 unanimously resolved in favor of joint Employer-Worker production councils. More significantly, the official Select Committee on National Expenditure has urged that "Management should take their workpeople more closely into their confidence." Even the *Financial News*, a business daily of the London City, says, "The workers feel that they have as much to contribute to the cooperative effort as those to whom managerial functions have been traditionally and exclusively assigned. There is force in the argument that managements as well as Labor have been 'diluted' by war conditions. There is room for new blood." Therefore the Management-Labor "production committee movement should be fostered and encouraged by both managements and government." The *Financial News* is progressive-conservative in the spirit of Minister of Information Brendan Bracken and his young Tory colleagues. Some employers have installed production councils with obvious benefit to themselves. But most manufacturers say No. They may see the wisdom of workers' participation in management now. They fear, however, that it could become a habit which will carry over into the post-war period. They are afraid of establishing embarrassing precedents. Even where the privileged classes refuse to think of the future of India or European federation, they do worry about the future of their ownership and control of the business of the country. They will not surrender their economic power.

One of the reasons for Labor's readiness to co-operate with management is the Excess Profits Tax which eliminates war profiteering or limits it to a low minimum. If the capitalists are working for the national good, Labor says, instead of for their own pockets, why not help them? The capitalists, on the other hand, are not always enthusiastic about the Excess Profits Tax.

The *Financial News* writes, "There is no doubt that the excess profits tax at the 100% level has been, and is, reducing output." This is serious, for the outcome of the present war "will be decided not on the playing fields of Eton but in the workshops of Birmingham and the industrial towns of Great Britain." But why should EPT reduce output? The *Financial News* contends that it destroys the incentive of the manufacturer, and the paper therefore demands a reduction of EPT to sixty or seventy per cent.

In this connection, the *Financial News* reveals a condition which is probably the most amazing thing I learned of during my stay in England. It says, "Given EPT concessions, however, coalowners would be readier to concentrate now on working the most productive seams. . . ." This means that since, owing to excess profit taxes, the coalowners cannot earn more money now by exploiting their better seams they are keeping those for after the war when the better the coal the more the profit and when not every kind of coal will sell as it does today. They are deliberately working their poorer seams. If this had not appeared black on white in a British "Wall Street" newspaper and if I had not received official confirmation that this practice exists I would not have believed it.

The coalowner who makes available his poorer coal for the war might give his son to the RAF to be killed. But because profits are low he saves his best seams for a day when there will be no ceiling on profits. The anomaly of this psychology struck the *Financial News*, and on one occasion it frankly named the motives which actuate British manufacturers in wartime. It listed love of country, hope of reward in the shape of elevation to the House of Lords as a peer, and fear of punishment. It classified them as the three P's: "Patriotism, the Peerage, and the Penitentiary." But what counts more than these, the newspaper added, is the fourth P, Profits.

I would add a fifth: Property. There are industrialists who forego excess profits for the sake of victory and their future as industrialists. It is wrong to suppose that even a majority of coalowners make reservations in their war effort because of EPT. But the surrender of profit is only temporary, whereas the loss of property would entail a permanent change of social status and the employers will fight that. In May, 1940, the month of Dunkirk, Parliament passed legislation empowering the government to conscript all men, women, and property. But now the emergency has passed, and a member of the War Cabinet told me that the May, 1940, legislation was merely intended as a threat to hold over the heads of recalcitrant or unco-operative owners. It has been used in isolated instances; some few factories have been taken over by the state. But when, in December, 1941, in connection with a new bill to widen the conscription age limits for men and women, an amendment was introduced in the House of Commons by George Russell Strauss, Aneurin Bevan, and Colonel Josiah Wedgwood, calling for "state control of key industries during war-time" it received only forty votes—forty out of six hundred possible votes in the House of Commons, when there are 166 labor M.P.'s in the House. Verily, the revolution is not just around the corner in England.

In another grave national emergency, of course, the movement for taking over industries may acquire a little more momentum. With the United States in the war and determined to equip its own armed forces first, the British must strive to step-up their production, and they will be impelled to inquire why, as John D. Biggers, special American government representative in Britain, said on his return from a trip to England, the British "are not getting the full production of which their plants are capable."

The problem is limited industrial capacity and, in the British Isles—as distinguished from the British Empire—limited manpower. Britain's factories and workers are inadequate for the successful waging of a war against the Axis powers. The army demands more men. The army, in fact, advertises in the press for factory workers. But the more men the army takes the more arms it needs and the fewer men there are in the factories to make them. It is like two people in a bed trying to keep warm under a narrow blanket. When one is covered the other gets uncovered. This is the key difficulty and it goes back several decades. Britain should have mechanized more after 1919. All of England's economic and political chickens came home to roost in 1939. Britain is paying a heavy price for muddling through the twenties and thirties. The shortcomings are primarily objective. They reside in physical conditions that cannot quickly be altered. But they are also in part subjective and are imbedded in the social thinking and economic instincts of the property owners and those in the government who think like them. The government still has no final plan for the distribution of manpower and womanpower between industry and the armed services. The Germans have a dual-purpose army. Coal miners work in the spring and summer and train or fight in the colder months when mining is difficult. When I asked the responsible official why England did not adopt this system he said, "We may be coming to something like that." Standardization of army equipment has not gone far enough. Machines needed by a manufacturer in the north of England stand idle in a factory in the south of England; coordination is cumbersome because of the different ownership of the two plants. If one firm improves its machinery the information is not always passed on to a second firm using similar machinery for munitions making; nobody helps his competitor with alacrity. Many articles of luxury or dispensable comfort are still being made in England. Further rationing would create greater equality, diminish grumbling about the privileged rich, and tend to curb inflationary tendencies. The Treasury sometimes doles out money like a miser. The ministry handing out contracts for planes often competes with the ministry handing out contracts for tanks or guns. (They do need one Ministry of Munitions.) Management wastes time and effort bidding for government work. Management wastes time and effort trying to operate so that the stockholders gain a profit. The government's commodity controllers are in many cases business men doing business in that commodity, and in no case has a Laborite received such a job.

Succinctly and trenchantly, Sir Richard Acland, Liberal M.P., has shown how British private interests clash with British public interests during this war. Speaking in the House of Commons in November, 1941, he said, "It is in our interest to postpone every postponable repair; it is in the interests of the owners to get every repair done and have it charged up to the Excess Profits Tax. It is in our interest to work the good seams in the coal mines now; it is in the owners' interest to postpone work on the good seams until after the war. It is in our interest to share trade secrets; it is in the owners' interest to preserve them. It is in our interest to concentrate output in every factory on one or few products; it is in their interests to keep the factory flexible by making as many different products as possible. It is in our interest that skilled men should spend part of their time teaching their skill to unskilled men; it is in the owners' interest that skilled men should be kept on direct production all the time. It is in our interest to save paper by cutting down advertising; it is in their interests to spend money which belongs to us—because otherwise it would go in Excess Profits Tax—in advertising things like aeroplane parts. . . . It is in our interest that women should replace men; it is in the interests of the firms to hang on to the men because they know that the women will go away after the war. It is in our interest that half-used machines should be sent to factories where they would be fully used; it is in the firms' interests to disguise the fact that the machines are half used. It is in our interest that skilled workers, when work falls off in one factory, should be sent to another factory; it is in the firms' interests to hang on to skilled workers in case a good order should turn up."

These conditions inspire frequent demands for more energetic government action towards the establishment of a real wartime economy. The British Conservatives hope they will somehow muddle through the war on their old industrial system. But even the British government's Select Committee on National Expenditure, reporting in September, 1941, complained that "the necessary transition from a peacetime economy is taking place too slowly, and more vigorous and far-reaching measures are now imperative." Amen. Those to whom property gives real power in Britain love the old. They think it has treated them well. As a matter of fact, it has weakened their country and got them into war.

The British achieved a miracle when they saved themselves from disaster in 1940. They did that singlehanded. They have grown stronger ever since. But the country is not secure without foreign aid. It is too weak industrially.

Britain remains the foremost and the most exposed anti-Nazi citadel. If it fell, victory over Hitler, Japan, and Italy would be delayed; it might never be won. America's participation in the war must therefore not be allowed to divert too much attention from Great Britain's urgent needs. England's morale is strong. England had strong defenses. But her military commitments are far-flung and varied, and the output of her factories is inadequate. She requires permanent aid from the United States. For England is America's permanent ally, permanent liability, and permanent asset. Whatever happens, Great Britain will be at the side of the United States in this war, and probably in the next peace. America's strength, Britain's shortcomings, Germany's ambitions, geography, and history have thrown England into the arms of the United States.

What about Russia?

WHAT WILL RUSSIA DO?

7. WHAT WILL RUSSIA DO?

Russia's fine fight has not reconciled me to Stalin's dictatorship any more than Germany's military victories reconciled me to the Hitler regime.

The Soviet nation has been fighting magnificently, better than most people, including most "experts," had expected. The "experts" miscalculated because they were misled by their prejudices and by the rapid Nazi blitzkrieg in France as well as by the difficulties of the Red Army in the invasion of Finland. If the Reichswehr crashed through the French Army and the Maginot Line in a few weeks, they reckoned, what chance had Russia? If Stalin took so long to smash tiny Finland, they reasoned, his army must be bad.

However, France was half-defeated before the war started, defeated by her own appeasers and near-fascists. France surrendered prematurely and unnecessarily when only part of her army had been engaged in battle and when her fleet and empire were intact and capable of continuing the struggle. France, therefore, should not have been used as a yardstick for Russia. Nor Finland. Moscow did not expect the Finns to resist. The first Soviet regiments which invaded Finland carried brass bands and propaganda leaflets. The Soviet government imagined that the Finnish proletariat would revolt and join the Bolsheviks. Only in the later stages of the war did the Red Army throw in its best troops and sufficient equipment to crack the Mannerheim Line. Moreover, Soviet soldiers did not put their heart into the fight against Finland. They had been educated as anti-imperialists, in the Lenin tradition. They did not understand why they should be invading little, unoffending Finland. Stalin himself, in a speech delivered in Moscow on November 6, 1941, explained that an army resisting an invader has a better morale than an army "waging a war of annexation, plundering a foreign country without any chance of believing even for a moment in the justice of its base cause." Stalin said this about the Nazi Army invading Russia. But the words also apply to the Soviet Army invading Finland.

Finland and France thus led observers into misjudging Russia's armed might.

I myself cautiously refrained from definite predictions about the length of the Soviet-Nazi war. In my articles I made none. In a broadcast over CBS on July 12, 1941, when Germany had already driven deep into Russian territory, I commented: "Russia cannot defeat Germany. But Germany can defeat Russia. Perhaps it will take Hitler longer than he had expected. Russia may parry the Nazi blow for three or four months. I imagine that Hitler would like nothing better than to deliver a speech from the top of the Lenin mausoleum on the Red Square in Moscow next November 7. Maybe he will. The other alternative is that Russia will hold back the Nazis and slow their advance. Hitler would then pursue his anti-Soviet war with increased intensity. To withdraw would mean a catastrophe for Nazism.

Hitler would go on. In that case, we will see a long bloody contest between Fascism and Bolshevism, a contest that will bring widespread ruin to the Soviet Union for it will be fought on Soviet soil. I think that if Russia has to fight for a long time, say for a year or more, it will grow progressively weaker."

The crucial fact about the Stalin-Hitler war is that, before attacking, Germany made no demands on Russia. There were no negotiations or conversations for months before the conflict opened. Hitler did not say to the Kremlin: I want you to give me so and so or else. . . . He said nothing. He did not offer Moscow a chance of bargaining or procrastinating or capitulating. He simply attacked. I know this from the British Foreign Office, from the United States State Department, and from the American Embassy in London. It is confirmed by Harry Hopkins, President Roosevelt's special envoy, in an article in the *American Magazine* for December, 1941, entitled "The Inside Story of My Meeting with Stalin." Hopkins writes: "When Hitler invaded Russia he did so without a word to Stalin, not a hint. In Moscow, in the Kremlin, this aroused a hatred of Hitler that nothing but the death of the German Chancellor could lessen." Russia fought Germany because she was attacked. Article 49 of the new Soviet Constitution provides that the Soviet government may go to war "in fulfilment of international treaty obligations for mutual aid against aggression," thus accepting the principle of going to war before an invasion. But Stalin chose to wait till the enemy came to Russia.

Why did Hitler wish to fight Russia? The key to

Hitler's strategy, in war as in diplomacy, is to "knock them out one by one." He knows that the Kaiser lost the war in 1918 because he had waged it on two major fronts. Hitler has always aimed, and still aims, to obviate the necessity of dividing his energy and attention between two fronts. He bribed Russia to stay out of the war in 1939 so that he could the more easily knock out France, Scandinavia, and the Balkan states and then turn on Russia. He would have been glad to bribe England to get out of the war in 1941 so that he could the more easily knock out Russia and then turn on England.

In 1941 Hitler saw the United States identifying itself to an increasing extent with England and coming closer to war. He anticipated what would be, in effect, an Anglo-American front in the west. Before that happened he wanted to destroy the possibility of a second front in the east, in Russia. Moreover, if he engaged Russia in Europe, Japan would not fear Russia in the Far East and Tokio would accordingly be encouraged to go to war and engage England and America on a second front in the Pacific area. The attack on Russia was thus designed to keep Germany out of a two-front war while creating a two-front war for Germany's enemies.

Hitler hoped to crush Russia and thereby make Nazi-Europe blockade-proof. Russia's raw materials and food resources, he calculated, would enable him to withstand the looming Anglo-American siege. And, with Russia under his control, he might ultimately lift that siege by a negotiated peace. He would say to England: "I am the master of Europe. You cannot defeat me. It is true I cannot invade you either. I cannot defeat you. Shall we go on bombing one another endlessly? Let us be sensible and talk peace." To America, after the proposed collapse of Russia, Hitler would have had a special message: "It is obvious now that England is powerless to win this war against a Germany which is the mistress of Europe. The only way I can be defeated is for you Americans to send an army of ten million men to invade the European continent. Do you want to do that for the sake of England? Do you want to do that after I have served humanity by annihilating Bolshevism?"

That was the Hitler plan.

But Hitler knew that his second world war could not be won in Russia. No matter how deep Hitler might have penetrated into Soviet Russia it would not have brought England to her knees. The only way to win the second world war was to invade and occupy the British Isles. Then why did not Hitler invade England? Why did he invade Russia instead?

The only possible answer is that he knew he could not invade England in 1941 and believed it would be easier to knock out Russia. The Nazi invasion of Russia was an *Ersatz*, or substitute, for the invasion of England. It was an admission on Hitler's part that he could not invade England; it was therefore an admission on Hitler's part that he could not win the war. He went into Russia to make sure, at least, of a draw. By success in Russia he hoped to achieve a stalemate and later, to compel a negotiated peace.

Suppose Hitler had not attacked Russia or England in the summer of 1941. He might have launched offensives against North Africa or the Near East. But in the meantime England would have been gaining strength and receiving more supplies from America. Russia would have been continuing her preparations. Some day, England, with intensified American aid, might take the offensive, first in the air, then on land. At such a juncture, Russia might have struck at Germany in the back. It is logical, therefore, that since Hitler could not invade England he had to invade Russia. He could not allow both to remain undisturbed.

Hitler could not invade Great Britain because the prerequisite of such an invasion is air superiority. If Hitler had enough oil to stage his vast offensives in Russia he had enough for an invasion of England. He lacked the air power. To invade Britain, the Germans would need air superiority over the English Channel while their first troops were crossing the English Channel, while the first German landing parties were groping for a hold on the British beaches, while these parties were seeking to expand their holds into bridgeheads, while they were attempting to penetrate inland, and while reinforcements were crossing the English Channel. The German Luftwaffe, in other words, would have to control the air over Britain for many days and nights, uninterruptedly. Ever since the Spring of 1941, however, the RAF has been so powerful that the Germans could not gain air superiority over any vital British area for one afternoon. The Luftwaffe could come and drop some bombs and run; but that is not air superiority. German fighter planes would have had to chase the RAF from the sky and stay in command of the air and protect the German invaders from bombing and strafing. That was impossible at any time in 1941.

I suspect that the practical intention of invading Russia, instead of England, first entered Hitler's mind in October, 1940, when the Nazi air blitzes failed to reduce the British fortress. The next month, Vyacheslav Molotov, then Prime Minister and Foreign Commissar of the Soviet government, arrived in Berlin. His meeting with Hitler was a fiasco, and it marks the beginning of the deterioration of Soviet-Nazi relations. The end of that deterioration was the outbreak of war between the two countries in June, 1941.

The spectacular fall of France in June, 1940, frightened Moscow. If the British succumbed, Russia was doomed. But British resistance encouraged Stalin to think that since Hitler would remain preoccupied in the west she would have to keep on good terms with Russia in the east. Just as Germany's plan to deal with western Europe in 1939 had permitted Stalin to acquire Polish and Baltic lands, so he now intended that Hitler's concentration on Britain would facilitate further Russian gains—this time in the Balkans. The Hitler-Molotov conversations, accordingly, dealt chiefly with the Balkans. Molotov presented Moscow's claims for new concessions in the Balkan peninsula. But Stalin had miscalculated. Hitler was going into the Balkans himself. The English nut could not be cracked. So Hitler decided upon a diversion into southeastern Europe.

In his proclamation announcing war on Russia in

June, 1941, Hitler revealed that Molotov, when he came to Berlin, had asked him four questions:

1. Would Germany act, if Russia made further moves against Rumania?
2. Would Germany help Finland, if Russia, which "again felt menaced by Finland," invaded that country a second time?
3. Would Germany mind if Russia gave a guarantee to Bulgaria and sent troops into Bulgaria?
4. Would Germany agree that Russia needed bases in the Dardanelles and the Bosporus?

Hitler sought to create the impression that in his replies to Molotov he had stood up for Rumania, Finland, Bulgaria, and Turkey and vetoed Soviet aggression against them. There is a story, but it too may be apocryphal, that a sensitive secret microphone had been installed in the room where Molotov talked with Hitler, and that the whole conversation was recorded and later reproduced by the Germans for the benefit of the Turks. The Turks, in any case, had information of their own regarding Moscow's designs on the Straits, and Soviet-Turkish relations had grown steadily worse since the Turkish Foreign Minister Saracoglu, visiting Moscow in October, 1939, began to suspect Stalin's interest in Turkish territory.

Molotov was no sooner out of Berlin than Hitler summoned pliant representatives of Hungary, Slovakia, and Rumania to Berlin and ordered them to join the Axis. They did. Moscow thereupon announced that Hungary had taken this step without Soviet approval. That is just the point. Hitler was demonstrating that he did not care to get Soviet approval. He had his own program of expansion into the Balkans. Hitler now increased his garrisons in Rumania and Hungary. He intensified the pressure on Bulgaria. The Kremlin made a wry face, but Hitler paid no attention. He occupied Bulgaria. Yugoslavia was next. Yugoslavia became the nub of the entire Soviet-Nazi relationship.

Germany started massing troops and equipment on the Russian frontier in February, 1941. I learned this from British and non-British sources in London whose information I have always accepted as a guide. In March, the Cvetkovitch government of Yugoslavia, dominated by Prince Paul, agreed to be "saved" by Hitler. But on March 27, a pro-British, if not British-instigated, revolt led by General Simovitch put King Peter on the Yugloslav throne. Germany thereupon attacked Yugoslavia. German army units already on the Russian border or in trains going to the Russian border were quickly shifted to Yugoslavia.

Stalin now saw in the Yugoslav affair an opportunity to cancel or at least postpone the attack on Russia. If Germany moved from Yugoslavia into Greece and then Crete and then perhaps into Syria, Palestine, Iraq, and Egypt, Russia would breathe more freely. It accordingly became important for Moscow to strengthen Yugoslavia. On April 5, 1941, therefore, the Soviet government signed a treaty of friendship with Yugoslavia. This was the high-water mark of overt Soviet opposition to Germany between the conclusion of the Soviet-Nazi pact on August 23, 1939 and the outbreak of the Soviet-Nazi war on June 22, 1941.

To the discomfiture of many prophets, however, Yugoslavia quickly collapsed under the Germans onslaught. The ink was scarcely dry on the Soviet-Yugoslav treaty when Yugoslavia crumbled.

The Kremlin knew immediately what to expect. On April 9, the Moscow *Red Star*, daily newspaper of the Red Army, wrote: "There can be no question of an invasion of Britain. The central burden of the war has been shifted from the west to the east." Shortly after Russo-German hostilities began, S. Lozovsky, the Soviet spokesman, told foreign correspondents in Moscow that on April 12 the German Luftwaffe opened a long series of reconnaissance flights over Soviet territory. Stalin understood what that meant. He ordered mobilization; the German invasion did not find the Russians offguard. On May 6, Stalin demoted Molotov and appointed himself Prime Minister of the Soviet Union. When the supreme emergency arrived he wished to be formally as well as actually in supreme command.

Nevertheless, Stalin still hoped that Hitler would invade Asia Minor instead of Russia. He still hoped to appease Hitler. Norway had been overrun by Germany in April, 1940. But the Norwegian minister remained in Moscow for more than a year and retained full diplomatic privileges. On May 9, 1941, the Soviet government withdrew those privileges. Belgium had been overrun by Germany in May, 1940. But the Belgian minister remained in Moscow for a whole year and retained full diplomatic privileges. On May 9, 1941 the Soviet government withdrew his privileges. Moscow was currying favor with Hitler. Stalin had just signed a

WHAT WILL RUSSIA DO? 149

treaty of friendship with Yugoslavia. The Yugoslavs had only just been defeated—partially defeated, as it turned out. Yet on May 9, Stalin also deprived the Yugoslav minister in Moscow of his diplomatic privileges. On May 12, moreover, Russia recognized the weak, flimsy government of Rashid Ali Beg Galiani, the pro-Nazi rebel of Iraq. Moscow was giving ample proof to Hitler of its readiness to behave.

But it was all in vain. On June 22, Hitler invaded Russia.

Soviet morale has been excellent throughout. In the middle of October, 1941, the Germans made a breakthrough near Moscow, and the Soviet capital seemed to become panicky. The Bolshevik radio, according to the *New York Times*, appealed to the Russian soldiers not to throw away their rifles; on October 15 and 16, the foreign diplomats, foreign correspondents, and many Soviet women, children, and officials were hastily evacuated from Moscow to Kuibishev. In those days too, as reported by the Soviet press, a Moscow factory director sent his workingmen home and said the Germans would soon be in the city; he was later executed. Except for this brief lapse, however—and it was speedily ended by rigorous Soviet measures—Russia's fighting spirit has, by all known symptoms, remained remarkably high.

There are several reasons. The intimacy of the Stalin and Hitler regimes during the Soviet-Nazi marriage was abhorrent to intelligent Bolsheviks and class-conscious Soviet citizens. They were pained to see their flag intertwined in Moscow with the Nazi swastika. They had been trained to detest fascism and Hitler, and they were shocked when, after the Soviet-Nazi pact, all anti-fascist propaganda disappeared from the Soviet press and radio. In fact, the official Moscow *Izvestia* said on October 9, 1939, that anti-Hitlerism was merely "a matter of taste"; you could or you could not be anti-Hitler. The Soviet propaganda machine attacked England, France, and America in those years, but not Nazi Germany. This entire phase of subservience to Hitler disgusted millions of good Leninists, and when it ended with Germany's assault on Russia there was relief in the heart. The attack released enthusiasm in Russia; the people, at last, could again be anti-fascist and fight fascism.

The vast bulk of the Soviet population was aroused by the invasion. No nation that believes in its future welcomes an invader. Most of western Russia, the Ukraine, and the Crimea had been occupied by Germany in 1918. The Germans killed and pillaged. The Russians remembered, and fought to prevent a repetition of that ordeal. Finally, the Russian peasant loves his land, and the Red Army is still a predominantly peasant army. Russians, even Russians who left Russia twenty and thirty years ago, have a deep attachment to the soil, the romance, the poetry of Russia.

In 1923, I went to study conditions in a Ukrainian village near Kharkov. Until 1917 all the land of the village had belonged to one family, the Rudenskys. Since then the Bolsheviks had nationalized this land. It belonged to the state, not to the Rudenskys. Nevertheless, the peasants of the village were worried lest the

Rudenskys some day return. They therefore followed the fate of each member of the family. The villagers themselves had murdered Rudensky and his wife when they seized the land. Two sons, officers in Denikin's "White" army, had died in the civil war. But one son had escaped, and they had heard that he was a waiter in Paris. Did I know him? They would have been more comfortable if he had been dead instead of washing dishes in a Montmartre restaurant.

The old landlords had tried to come back into Soviet Russia in 1918, 1919, and 1920 in the wake of the "White" Russian anti-Soviet armies. Perhaps the old landlords, or new landlords, would arrive with the Nazis. The peasants do not wish to see landlords reestablished in Russia. Many peasants have become reconciled to collectivized agriculture. They may not have liked it in the beginning; many may have obstructed it. But it had proved to be a wise reform even though the cost in lives was excessive. In any case, collectives were better than landlords. The peasants stood like an iron wall against Hitler. The workers did not like fascism. Nor did the intellectuals and officials. Communists, trade-union leaders, government office-holders, and many others knew that a Hitler victory would mean their death. All of them fought for the good that was in the Soviet regime, not for the bad. The morale in Russia has been good because of that good and despite the bad. It has been good despite Stalin more than because of Stalin. It has been good because the people hope that in victory Russia will become better.

In addition to spirit, the Red Army also had plenty

of trained men and vast accumulations of arms. For ten years the Soviet regime, wisely, had been making these accumulations. Stalin said in a speech on November 6, 1941, that the Germans were better supplied with tanks and planes than the Russians. But the Russians had large numbers of these and other arms else they would not have been able to cope with Nazi attacks. The Russians, beside, are more accustomed than the Germans to the bitter cold weather of the murderous winter of their country.

These, it would seem, are sufficient reasons for the splendid military performance of the Soviet armed forces. But certain persons refuse to let it go at that. They have dragged in another circumstance. They try to use the excellent fighting of the Red Army in order now, belatedly, to justify the Stalin purge and the Moscow trials. One of the worst sinners—because he ought to know better—is Mr. Joseph E. Davies, who occasionally visited Russia when he was United States ambassador to Moscow. He explains Russia's ability to withstand the German attack by Stalin's timely elimination of Russia's "Fifth Column."

It has frequently been asserted that the Soviet generals and officers whom Stalin ordered to be executed in the big army purge of 1937 were in collusion with Germany and Japan. It has been asserted; it is easy to make assertions. But not even the Soviet government, let alone Mr. Davies or any of its foreign partisans, has ever adduced one iota of evidence to prove that the generals and their subordinates were traitors to the Soviet Union. Assertions, yes; but no proof.

On June 11, 1937, a secret Soviet court-martial passed death sentences on Marshal Tukhachevsky, the leading general of the Red Army, and seven other generals of the very highest rank. A ninth general, Gamarnik, was reported to have committed suicide when the G.P.U. came to arrest him.

An official bulletin published the next day stated that all the eight generals had confessed to the crimes charged against them. But we do not know whether they actually confessed. The public was not admitted to the trial. No foreigners were present. No record of the trial, no excerpt from the record, has ever been made public. We only have the Soviet communiqué stating that they confessed. That cannot be regarded as convincing evidence.

Tukhachevsky and his generals were tried by their "peers." But most of the trial judges, generals all, were subsequently executed themselves. Did they know too much? Did they know that there never was a trial or that there never were any confessions? Did they know whether or not Gamarnik committed suicide, and, if he committed suicide, did they understand why?

I undertook to show in my previous book, *Men and Politics*, that even in the public Moscow trials of civilian Bolshevik leaders the confessions were untrustworthy. Other writers have done likewise. If public confessions are open to doubts, can any serious person credit confessions reportedly made in a secret court-martial?

The logic of some persons is as follows: The Russians are fighting well. The Russians had a purge. Therefore the Russians are fighting well because they had a purge. An equally silly syllogism would be: The Russians are fighting well. The Russians had a famine. Therefore the Russians are fighting well because they had a famine.

The RAF has fought well and has saved England. Is that because it was purged? The Greek army stoutly resisted the Italians and, though hopelessly outnumbered, bravely carried on against the Nazis. Is that explained by a Greek purge? Can an army fight well only after its generals have been shot?

A purge may be desirable in certain circumstances. The Spanish Civil War of 1936-39 might have been averted if the republican government had effectively purged General Franco and a handful of his disloyal generals before the revolt started. But those generals came from a class that was, by tradition and self-interest, hostile to the progressive republican government. The same cannot be proved of the purged Soviet leaders. To expand Spain's experience into a principle would be to say that all generals everywhere are traitors and should be liquidated. Each case should be examined on its merits.

Rather than claim that the Red Army fought well because its best generals were shot, one might suggest that the Red Army would have fought even better if Tukhachevsky, a recognized military genius, and his able colleagues had lived to lead the Soviet forces into battle against the Nazis.

There is no need of sugar-coating Anglo-American collaboration with Russia by attempting to justify the purges and the Stalin terror. During my stay in England in 1941, London had only one minor air raid and the entire country, in general, was free from bombs; the German Luftwaffe was busy in Russia. The Russians have killed, wounded, and captured several million Germans, and that is reason enough for wishing to prolong Russia's resistance whether Stalin goes to church or not. By a chain of circumstances not of his own making, Stalin is fighting on the side of the "angels," and if the "angels" want to win they would do well to aid Stalin. I suspect the anti-Hitlerism of any person or institution that opposes Anglo-American collaboration with Moscow. I wonder how intense is the desire of that person or institution to see Hitler defeated. But this is no reason for going into contortions in order to prove that Stalin loves God and would never, God forbid, harm a fly, let alone an innocent general. There is no use trying to whitewash Stalin in the blood of millions of Russian soldiers who have fought in this war. Blood does not whitewash. Tens of thousands of young Russian men in a fine generation which I saw grow to maturity in Russia are now dead or maimed because Stalin, to further his personal political ambitions, deprived the Red Army of its best talent.

Another cause of Russia's troubles in the Russo-German war was Stalin's anti-Litvinov foreign policy. In the perspective granted by events, it is now possible to see that, as this second world war approached, the ideal Soviet policy—ideal from the viewpoint of Soviet territorial interests—would have been not to sign a pact with Hitler, nor to enter into an agreement with England

and France, nor to engage in aggression against Poland, the Baltic states, Finland, and Rumania. Russia should have remained neutral—until France was attacked in June, 1940, and then intervened to save France. The way the Red Army has been fighting it is obvious that Russia's entry into the European war in the summer of 1940 would have diverted so much German military strength as to have given France a good chance to survive. It was the Russian offensive in Eastern Prussia in 1914 that saved France on the Marne. Soviet Russia, however, did not move when Hitler struck at France. While the fighting was still proceeding, the Moscow radio, broadcasting in French, gave the French people a gloomy picture of their chances in the war. Moreover, Moscow, by its instructions to the Communist parties of France, England and other victims of Nazi aggression, facilitated Hitler's conquests everywhere in Europe. One European nation after the other fell into Hitler's lap; then no one remained on the continent except Germany and Russia, and Germany attacked Russia, and Russia, alone, had to bear the full brunt of an undivided German military assault.

Some have contended that, but for the bargain which Moscow and Berlin reached in August, 1939, Hitler would have invaded Russia in 1939. He would have seized Poland and then pushed on into Soviet territory, it is argued. The simplest answer to this argument is: why didn't he? The pact itself was no protection for Russia. The pact was a piece of paper. England and France had declared war on Germany, but England had limited her war effort to bombing Germany with paper pamphlets and France had taken the offensive and captured a few trees in the forest between the Nazi and French lines. If Hitler had wished to attack Russia in 1939 he could have done so. But he apparently trusted the Russians more than he did the Anglo-French forces and he therefore decided to crush the western powers first. Maxim Litvinov, Soviet ambassador to Washington, made this clear in his broadcast from Moscow on July 8, 1941. Hitler, he said, "intended first to deal with the western states so as to be free afterwards to fall upon the Soviet Union." That being the case, Stalin should have helped the western states so that Hitler would not have been free afterwards to fall upon the Soviet Union. It was Stalin's great historic blunder not to have done this.

Litvinov, whom a high State Department official described to me recently as "the most consistent European statesman over the last twenty years," explained in his Moscow broadcast exactly what happened. "There was a hitch somewhere," he said. England did not fall. "Hitler has not the training for a Channel swimmer yet. And so another plan matured in his brain. . . . He decided to have a lightning war in the east." Litvinov, unwavering champion of collective security, always saw the European conflict in the right light. But Stalin repeatedly miscalculated, and a statesman has no right to be wrong. In the hard-boiled game of international politics, a policy is judged by results. If Stalin could have kept his country permanently at peace then he might have been warranted in reaching a bargain with Hitler. But he only succeeded in getting his country into war under the worst conditions when there was no army on the European continent to create a second front and when Germany had the industries of the conquered countries to make arms for her use against the Soviet army. Hitler used new French tanks, and Czech tanks, against Russia. Russia's benefits from the marriage with Hitler—territories occupied and time gained—were illusory. The time was more valuable to Hitler than to Stalin, and the elimination of the buffer territories between Germany and Russia was a disaster to Russia. It antagonized the peoples of the Baltic countries and brought Finland into the war against Russia. Just as the fascist, pro-German Greek dictator Metaxas defended his nation's independence against Italian and Nazi encroachment so it is probable, and I think certain, that if the Russians had not invaded Finland in 1939, the Finns, Mannerheim notwithstanding—he was not dictator of Finland—would have refused to assist Germany in June, 1941. But a Finland embittered by the Russian attack, weakened by it, and hoping to recover lost territories from Russia, succumbed more easily to Hitler's pressure and blandishments. The participation of Finland and Rumania in the German war against Russia was made a thousand times more certain by Russia's earlier aggression against them. Their military activity against Russia cost Russia far more than Russia gained through the aggression.

The simple fact is that appeasement and truck with the inevitable fascist enemy did not pay France or England or America or Russia. Appeasement never pays. On the contrary, France and England have paid dearly for appeasing Japan in China, Mussolini in Abyssinia, Hitler and Mussolini in Spain, and Hitler in Czechoslovakia. The United States sold oil and scrap iron to Japan. Then Japanese aeroplanes with that oil in their motors dropped bombs made of that scrap iron on American warships and American possessions. Similarly, Russia has paid for giving Hitler a one-front war in 1939 and 1940, for selling him oil, grain, and other commodities, and for crushing the very same small nations which Stalin had publicly, in March, 1939, promised to defend against attack.

The Soviet-Nazi war has apparently been the bloodiest and most expensive war in the history of mankind. Figures issued by either side on their own or the enemy's casualties cannot be regarded as final or reliable. But Germans as well as Soviet losses have undoubtedly been very high. To date, the Soviet army has made the greatest contribution to the fall of Hitler. The British defeated Napoleon, but actually Napoleon was defeated in Spain and Russia. Hitler may also be losing the second world war in Russia.

Checked by Moscow's stout defenses and by the cold which froze his soldiers' fingers, feet, noses and ears and handicapped the Luftwaffe's flights, Hitler's strategy for Russia nevertheless remained unaltered. It consists of the intensification of Germany's arms output to replenish supplies depleted in the fighting in Russia, continued pressure on Russia unless Stalin accepts peace or agrees to a tacit truce, continued attacks on the British Empire and American islands so as to curtail Anglo-American arms deliveries to Russia, and Turkish or Japanese military co-operation against the Soviet regime. If Germany and Japan could together annihilate Russia, Germany would be in a position to give Japan active assistance in China and in the whole Pacific area. That of course would make Germany the neighbor of Japan and many Japanese may not relish the prospect. But the entire Axis concept of victory presupposes Germany's penetration into Asia and thus Japan's subordination to Germany. To counteract Hitler's anti-Soviet plans, which are also plans against America, England, and China, the democracies should therefore, for their own good, intensify collaboration with and arms deliveries to Russia, and seize the initiative in all theatres of the war.

But suppose the democratic allies win the war, and suppose Russia is one of the victors. Does that not raise the specter of Russian domination of Europe and the spread of Communism throughout the world?

Men change their views and goals. So do governments. It is a serious but not infrequent error to believe that because the name remains the same the character is the same. Napoleon committed many reprehensible acts in the name of the French Revolution. How many crimes had been committed in the name of democracy? In a dictatorship, the will of the dictator counts for a great deal. Otherwise he would not be dictator. That is why a dictatorship is subject to sharper detours of policy than a plodding stabilized democracy in which the need of obtaining popular assent or at least popular understanding militates against sudden zigzags of government

WHAT WILL RUSSIA DO?

policy. Stalin has often completely reversed Soviet practice without ever offering the public an explanation.

Fundamental shifts of policy have taken place in Moscow in recent years, especially since 1935. These put a very different face on the Soviet regime. There has been a steady departure from socialist or Communist ideals and a gradual trend towards un-Bolshevik nationalism.

The Bolshevik revolution of 1917 was an attack on Russia. Bolshevism aimed to remove the ugly physical and cultural vestiges of Czarism and to build something new and better. In many respects, it succeeded. Agriculture has been modernized. Vast new plants and new cities have sprung up. There are more schools, universities, roads, bridges, libraries and printing presses. But while creating a new physical mold Stalin accepted and perfected most of the worst features of the Czarist terror. Oppression is worse in Russia today than it was under the Czar. And it is oppression not of anti-Soviet persons, who are few and far between; it is oppression of Soviet persons. Moreover, Stalin has turned away from Leninist internationalism and refurbished the old Russian nationalism.

The revolution was an attempt to graft socialism on backward Russia. It was a struggle between Karl Marx and Peter the Great. At times, Marx had the upper hand. Today, Peter is on top. Peter was the Russian and the builder; he was crude, cruel, and ruthless as well as unorthodox. He used the knife and the ax to teach the nation "culture." Peter is Stalin's hero. Indeed, reflecting Stalin's taste for ancient czars, the official Moscow *Izvestia* of March 19, 1941, made a strong plea for a reinterpretation of Ivan the Terrible's character and role in history. He was not so terrible, we now learn.

Since 1935, the Bolsheviks have rewritten Czarist Russia's history to make it more palatable to a Soviet generation which had earlier been taught to abominate the pre-revolutionary past under the absolute monarchy. Stalin had a new policy and so Russia had to have a new history to fit that policy. In similar fashion, revolutionary history has been rewritten. The new policy aimed to establish continuity between the Czarist and Bolshevik chapters of Russia's history so as to give the Russian a sense of pride in being part of a nation that has a long and glorious record.

Stalin's swing towards nationalism makes an interesting theoretical commentary on Bolshevism. The outstanding tendency of Bolshevism is disruptive. It arouses class against class and it gave each of the numerous national minorities in the Soviet Union a separate individuality. That did not make for cohesion. Soon after Hitler came into office in Germany, the faint beginnings of a new trend were discernible in Moscow, and in 1935, and then in ever-greater crescendo, the new Stalin line made itself manifest. Reactionary Czarist generals long dead were redecorated and displayed as Russian national heroes. Moscow started talking about "our Ukrainian and White Russian blood brothers." An emphasis on blood and ethnic origin is distinctly out of tune with Communism which stresses not blood but class, profession, and social origin. The Russian language, the national tongue of only a minority of the Soviet population—the majority consists of Ukrainians, Armenians, Georgians, Tatars, Kazaks, and a hundred other racial groups—was paraded as the one great language of the country, and more pressure was put on non-Russian Soviet inhabitants to study and speak it. "We love our great, strong and picturesque Russian language," Soviet propaganda said. That was a definite divorce from the Leninist attitude towards national culture; it was an approach to the Czarist attitude. New words appeared in the Soviet lexicon: homeland, fatherland, motherland.

Perhaps Stalin had decided that socialism without nationalism made it more difficult to govern Russia.

The Soviet press and radio never speak of "Nazi Germany." They refer to Germany as "Hitlerite Germany." During my stay in England recently I learned that Soviet representatives sought to persuade the British Broadcasting Corporation likewise to drop the word "Nazi" and use "Hitlerite" instead. This has more than a superficial significance. "Nazi" stands for National Socialist, and Stalin does not like that term to be applied to Germany. In his speech on November 6, 1941, Stalin said: "Is it possible to regard the Hitlerites as nationalists? This is impossible. In actual fact, the Hitlerites now are not nationalists but imperialists. . . . Can Hitlerites be regarded as socialists? No! This is impossible. In actual fact, the Hitlerites are sworn enemies of socialists, out-and-out reactionaries and plunderers." So Stalin rejects Hitler's right to call himself a National Socialist. Stalin has himself stated that in the Soviet Union, the culture of racial minorities like

Armenians, Turkomans, and so forth is "Nationalist in form and Socialist in content." Stalin, in effect, says to Hitler: The term National Socialism belongs to me; you cannot use it. But the original Bolshevik conception was International Socialism.

From Stalin's new emphasis on Russian nationalism it was one step to Slavism, the cult of the Czars. Simultaneously, the revolution and the world proletariat were mentioned with diminishing frequency in Soviet publications and speeches.

In this soil lies the root of Russia's aggression in 1939 and 1940. Nationalism, Slavism, and aggression are the tight links of one chain. One of the main reasons for Stalin's vast purge was his desire to get rid of the old Bolsheviks and stalwart Leninists who would have hated his radical departures from Lenin's teachings. The other central reason for the purge was Stalin's wish to remove all those whom he considered potential rivals and all those who never believed that he was the infallible, omniscient, one-and-only leader.

With the outbreak of the Soviet-Nazi war, the trend towards race and away from class ideology was speeded up. In years gone by, before the ascendancy of Stalinist nationalism, the Third International, or Comintern, would issue proclamations on the slightest provocation. A strike in Java, a speech by a British minister, a visit of a British naval squadron to Riga or Rumania became a threat of war to the Soviet Union, and the Comintern called the workers of the world to defend the Soviet Union; "Hands Off Soviet Russia," was the usual slogan. But in June, 1941, Hitler actually laid rough hands on Russia. A fascist nation made war on the Soviet Union. Yet the Comintern was absolutely silent. No proclamation or manifesto has come from its offices. Georgi Dimitrov, the head of the Comintern, has a tremendous reputation in Germany and in many other countries. At the Reichstag fire trial in Leipzig he acquitted himself nobly and defied the mighty Goering in the witness box. Did Dimitrov go to the Moscow microphone and appeal to German workers to revolt? Not a word has come from Dimitrov since the Nazi invasion of Russia though he had denounced England, France, and America in 1939 and 1940. No international workers' conference or congress of the Comintern has been convened in Moscow to adopt plans for action in this great Soviet emergency. Instead, a Slav congress was summoned in Moscow. It was addressed by Alexei Tolstoi, a Soviet writer of noble birth and author of a novel about Peter the Great. Tolstoi called Moscow "the heart of Slavdom." It had once been hailed as the heart of the world proletariat. Fascism, he said, wishes "to enslave and exterminate the Slav world." It had previously been excoriated for aspiring to enslave the workers and dominate the whole world.

Professor Derzhavin, a member of the Soviet Academy of Science, stated on October 3, 1941, that "Fascism is the worst foe of Slavism." At the September, 1941, session of the Academy of Science history section it was affirmed that "the whole history of the Slav peoples has passed under the sign of a stubborn war for freedom and independence against the Teutons. . . . The destruction of Hitlerism will lead to the national, political and cultural renaissance of the Slavonic nations." That is where Moscow is tending. It is interested in the Slavs of Bulgaria, Serbia, and Poland. Some weeks ago the Moscow radio appealed to the Red Army to fight with undiminished vigor. "We are fighting," it said, "for the right to breathe, for our children, for our fatherland, for Russia." Not for socialism. Not for revolution. Not for democracy. Similar words might have been used by Czarist Russia, by Nazi Germany, or by any capitalist state.

The metamorphosis which these words and sentiments reflect is the most important thing that has happened in Soviet politics since 1935. It is little noticed because it is subtle and slow. But it is also very profound. It is altering the very fiber of the Soviet regime.

What, then, would be Russia's appeal to outside countries in case of a victory of the allied democracies? She might call them to join the Slav motherland for protection against the Germans. But the Germans, presumably, would have been defeated. And the "little Slav brothers" of Bulgaria, Serbia, and Poland might fear the crushing embraces of the "big Slav brother." For leftists in advanced western countries, Soviet Russia might have the attraction of a country that had destroyed private capitalism. But the chief concern of the workingmen and intellectuals of the major capitalist countries is how and what to build in place of capitalism destroyed, and here Russia offers the dreary picture of bloody personal dictatorship, complete suppression of civil rights, discouragement of thought, blind unquestioning obedience to the ukases of an omnipotent leader, crushing of personality, boundless insecurity—for nobody's job or social position or person is safe in a dictatorship—and the same old race nationalism that has plagued Europe.

I do not think Russia would attract with her beauty or attract by her magnetism.

Judged not by hysterical outcries but by the open book of history, Soviet Russia never had either military or political offensive power before this war started. The Soviet Union was less of a menace to India, for instance, than Czarist Russia, and neither the British Empire nor British capitalism was ever exposed to any threat from Soviet Russia. Actually, the activity of the small British Communist party strengthened British capitalism by making British Labor anti-Communist. Nowhere in the world did the Communist parties of capitalist countries undermine the foundations of the social system and set themselves up as an alternative. To the limited extent to which Communists outside of Russia have achieved success it has always been when they joined non-Communist and anti-Communist groups to further a non-Communist objective. Examples are the work for Loyalist Spain, the Popular Front of 1935-1939, and defense measures in the democracies after June 22, 1941. But whenever the Communists pursue their own goal—revolution to be followed by the establishment of a Communist state—they are dismal failures and cannot be taken seriously.

But could Russia, after this war, impose herself by force on the weakened European nations? This seems improbable, simply because, after the tremendous expenditure by Russia of energy, manpower, and material in the present war and in view of the vast ruin in Russia, she will lack the necessary strength for military, economic, or political expansion.

Even if Germany suddenly collapsed from within in the near future, and the Red Army, still intact, occupied the country, it is unlikely that Russia would be able to feed, clothe, and reconstruct Germany or supply Germany with the raw materials needed to employ her population. Throughout the revolution, Russia has failed adequately to feed, clothe, and house her own citizens, and the strain of war has already been so heavy that it is extremely doubtful whether Russia would have any surpluses with which to restore Germany and neighboring countries or prevent them from starving.

Should Hitler continue to wage war against Russia for another year or two and then go down in defeat it is altogether out of the question that Russia would have the physical strength to attempt the occupation of Germany and Nazi-occupied lands. That would be a major military and economic operation which the Soviets could not undertake. Soviet occupation of Germany and other parts of eastern Europe would stir class passions, national hates, and fears of permanent annexation. The inhabitants would be resentful and disaffected especially since the Russians could not send food, clothing, raw material, engineers, and organizing personnel.

After this war, assuming the defeat of the Fascist International, Russia will have her own urgent problems. It is one of the bitterest tragedies in man's memories that so many of the results of the several Soviet

Five Year Plans—the new cities, factories, dams, roads, homes, schools, and recreational facilities—should have been smashed by Hitler's legions riding hither and yon over the face of Russia. The great Soviet peoples invested their health, nerves, and the lives of many of their citizens to build a new future, and, then an invader came, and in a few months what had been purchased at such high cost was ground into dust. The Soviet nation, when hostilities cease, will have to muster the faith and stamina to go to work and do it all over again. The Soviet peoples are capable of that. I have seen their startling resilience and recuperative powers. But it will require all they have to prevent Russia from lapsing into turmoil and chaos. They will have little excess energy to devote to holding down and building up large foreign countries.

It is a much safer assumption that those countries, now fascist or fascist-dominated, will look to rich America for food and aid in reconstruction. On the day when Hitler is defeated there will be British and American armies on the European continent which will have accomplished that defeat, and these will temporarily make their presence felt in Germany and prepare the way for the economic assistance which only the United States will be in a position to grant in sufficient measure to permit Europe to settle down and live in prosperity again.

The penetration of a nationalist Russia into western and central Europe would mean incessant strife and tension for the tired millions. Having lived through years of combat and taut nerves they will not be drawn towards a system that promised an indefinite period of the same sort of thing. An enlightened American policy of co-operation with the progressive democratic elements in Europe would open a much brighter prospect of relaxation and peace than would Russian expansion.

Europe will prefer America to Russia.

AMERICA'S NEW ROLE IN
WORLD AFFAIRS

8. AMERICA'S NEW ROLE IN WORLD AFFAIRS

THE UNITED STATES is the richest and most powerful nation in the world. America has reached a stage in its development and consciousness which would enable it to assume world leadership.

Germany is striving for world domination. America refuses to be dominated by Germany. That is the chief issue for America in the present war. Even prior to Japan's attack on the United States, the second world war had become a contest between Germany and America, with England playing the role of America's partner—senior partner in age, junior partner in importance.

The United States was committed to a German defeat long before December 7, 1941, when Japanese planes bombed Hawaii. That was the national policy approved by Congress and implemented by the Lease-Lend Act and the repeal of parts of the Neutrality Law. The United States government had, with the obvious approval of the country, appropriated thirteen billion dollars for the manufacture of arms which were to be delivered, without payment, to the nations fighting the Hitler Axis. No nation had ever done such a thing. No nation would ever do it simply for the love of another nation. We do not love the British thirteen billion dollars' worth.

In international politics altruism is scarce, and what looks like charity is merely the long view of selfish ends. The very term "Aid to Britain" was an unhappy one; it tended to register in the subconscious the idea that this is somebody else's war.

It was America's war from the very beginning. America helped Britain because that helped America. While England fought Germany, the United States could not be attacked by Germany. If Britain defeated Germany, neither Germany nor Japan would for a long time be able to attack the United States. Therefore, America wished to help Britain defeat Germany.

That was the strategy of "Aid of Britain."

Of course, some Americans said America could never be attacked; therefore we need not help Britain. Until the night before bombs rained on Pearl Harbor, isolationists and non-interventionists were assuring the American people that since the Germans had failed to cross the English Channel, which was only twenty miles wide, nobody could cross the two oceans that protected us. Then the Japanese crossed 3,800 miles of ocean to attack Hawaii. Until December 6, isolationists and non-interventionists were assuring the American people that it did not matter if Britain fell. It did not matter whether Russia held out. We would be safe if Germany won the war. We would be safe even if we stood alone, the isolationists declared. But on December 7, 1941, Germany had not won; Japan still had the British and the Dutch to contend with in the Far East.

We were not alone. And yet the Japanese dared to make a frontal attack on America. How secure would America have been if British power in Europe and Asia had crumbled and if Russia did not engage a large part of Germany's forces?

Among the isolationists there were sincere pacifists and idealistic socialists with 1910 notions of the world. But the bulk of them were misguided reactionaries who were too blinded by anti-Rooseveltism to see the dangers facing America, and too pro-fascist (Hitler to them was the wave of the future) to want to fight fascism. These people performed a distinct disservice to the United States by interfering with the public's understanding of the issues in this war. These people are still with us—and reactionaries change their spots less frequently than leopards.

They perverted the facts. They said the British and French were interventionists and thereby brought this war upon themselves. The British and French, however, did not intervene in China. They were isolationists in Abyssinia, Spain, Austria, and Czechoslovakia. In each case, Hitler, Hirohito, and Mussolini got exactly what they wanted. But they did not stop. Nonintervention encouraged them to ask for more until they succeeded in dragging the whole world into war.

In a famous article, reprinted in full in the *New York Times* of November 10, 1941, Dr. Paul Joseph Goebbels, Nazi Propaganda Minister, confessed that "Europe's problems would not have been solved had Poland in the summer of 1939 renounced Danzig and granted Germany a passage through the Corridor, or had England and France, following the victorious termination of the Polish campaign, been willing to discuss the Fuehrer's peace offer. We would still have had to take up arms in a few years." In other words, even if England and France had not intervened when Hitler attacked Poland, even if they had signed a negotiated peace over Poland as they did over Czechoslovakia, Germany would still have launched a second world war. That is what the Nazis think of the idea of negotiated peace which the isolationists loved so dearly.

There was one negotiated peace. Hitler negotiated it with Chamberlain at Munich in September, 1938. It gave Hitler what he asked. It lasted eleven months. There was another negotiated peace. Stalin negotiated it with Hitler on August 23, 1939. It served Hitler's purpose. It lasted twenty-two months.

The British and French isolationist non-interventionists and the American isolationist appeasers failed to grasp that if the democracies had intervened to save the early victims of fascist aggression they might have saved themselves from fascist aggression. The second world war was not inevitable. It might have been averted by far-sighted policies and timely acts.

Displaying a remarkably sympathetic understanding for the enemies of their countries, the appeasers justified Japan's invasion of Manchuria. Japan needed raw materials and areas in which to colonize her excess population, they said. Ditto for Mussolini in Abyssinia. And Austria—well, Austria was German, wasn't it? And the Sudetenland was German. And it was only fair to give Hitler Danzig. Chamberlain conceded that China was the natural field for Japanese expansion, and he told the House of Commons that Germany had a right to a special position in the Balkans.

There never was a greater hoax than the justification of fascist aggression on the ground that the world was divided into "haves" and "have-nots." Mussolini seized Abyssinia. Did he stop to exploit its economic wealth? No; he used the money he might have applied to that purpose to invade Spain immediately after the Abyssinian campaign was over. And then he occupied Albania, and then he laid claim to Nice, Savoy, and Tunis.

Austria was a rich haul. Did Hitler stop to develop its industrial and commercial possibilities? No; Austria made it strategically easier for him to pluck the Sudetenland. So six months after Austria he engineered Munich. Did he stop to develop the business of the Sudetenland? No; the fall of the Sudetenland deprived the rump of Czechoslovakia of vital strength. Therefore Hitler took all of Czechoslovakia. Czechoslovakia is one of the richest countries of Europe. Did Hitler build it up? No; he got Czechoslovakia in March, 1939, and the next month he wheeled his army around and began to threaten Poland. In September, 1939, he invaded Poland.

Likewise Japan. Manchuria is a vast country. The Japanese had no sooner annexed it than they invaded the five northern provinces of China, and very soon they attacked central China, and then Indo-China and then Thailand.

In no single case was the primary compulsion for

fascist expansion economic. The Axis nations were not after raw materials. They were after war materials. It was not enough for them to be able to buy supplies. They wanted to own them so they could use them for attacks on their enemies and deny them to their enemies.

Hitler had the industrial equipment, the labor, the German money, and the foreign currency to create history's most powerful military machine. If he had applied those resources to Germany's civilian needs the nation would have been strong and prosperous. But that was not his goal. Nor was it the goal of the Japanese and Italians.

The fascist goal was world domination. China, Abyssinia, Spain, Austria, and Czechoslovakia were the stepping stones to world domination. The appeasers did not wish to understand this.

The totalitarians had decided that the democracies were old, senile, flabby, decadent, and weak-willed. They had decided that this was an opportunity, which comes once in several centuries, to drive Britain, America, Holland, and Belgium from their commanding position in the world. They had decided that they themselves would rule the world to the exclusion of others. That is what Hitler calls the New Order.

Mussolini never seized power in Italy. The "March on Rome" of which the fascists boast never took place. Mussolini rode to Rome in a Pullman sleeper and the weak King and the pusillanimous prime minister of Italian democracy meekly handed over the reins of office to Mussolini so that he could imprison and kill

Italian democrats and destroy Italian democracy. Small wonder that Mussolini learned to hold democrats in contempt.

Hitler never seized power in Germany. There was no revolutionary coup. In January, 1933, Hitler was on the downgrade. He was losing votes. The Nazi tide, observers said, was running out. Just at that juncture, the president and chancellor of democratic Germany made a deal with Hitler and presented him with power. German democracy abdicated to fascism so that the fascists could pack the democrats into concentration camps and shoot them and crush democratic institutions. Small wonder that Hitler had no respect for democrats.

Having seen how easy it had been to overthrow democracy at home, the fascists decided they could deal in like manner with world democracy. They tried in Abyssinia and it worked. They tried in Spain and it worked. They tried and tried and it worked and worked again. And so they were sure that this was a unique chance to topple over the democracies and make themselves masters of the world.

That is the origin of this second world war.

This war is a war for world mastery launched by a league of fascist powers with Nazi Germany as conductor. The Japanese attack on America is part of a larger struggle. President Roosevelt, in his Bill of Rights speech on December 16, 1941, put the entire emphasis on Hitler as the enemy, and in his December 15, 1941, report to Congress on Lease-Lend operations he did not even mention Japan but did state that "We are now engaged in a total war against a group of Axis powers led by Nazi Germany and bent on world domination."

How could Germany achieve world domination, however, while America was strong and independent? That would not have been world domination. It is for this reason that political analysts who had watched world developments since the beginnings of totalitarian aggression were sure that America, the great obstacle to Nazi world ascendancy, was in danger. Just as Abyssinia and Spain were preliminaries to the attack on Britain, just as Czechoslovakia was the preliminary to the invasion of France, so the war on France and England was the prologue to a Nazi contest with the United States.

When Japan started her conquest of China in 1931 some innocents believed that Japan would allow American finance and business to co-operate in the upbuilding of China. They know now they were wrong. Japan closed the open door in America's face. When Mussolini invaded Abyssinia, Englishmen said this was not very serious; he would have to come to the London City—"cap in hand" was the expression used—for the money with which to exploit that backward African colony. They know now they were wrong. Mussolini intended to exploit it himself. The purpose of Axis aggressions was to drive out the democracies and keep them out.

If, therefore, Hitler had won this war before America entered it he would have dominated Europe, Asia, and Africa in association with his fascist accomplices. He would have hung shingles on those continents reading "Democracies Stay Out." That would have meant America. He would also have made use of the Spanish Falange to spread anti-American, anti-democratic views in the U. S. A.'s not-always-so-democratic "good neighbors" to the south.

Hitler would have kept the United States out of the eastern hemisphere and competed with us in parts of the western hemisphere. The United States is a young, virile, expanding nation. Hitler would have told America to stay at home, to curtail production, to restrict trade, and to stop growing.

Hitler is a challenge to America's growth and to America's future. Some Americans knew this with their intelligence and told others. Some knew it with their instincts. That, apart from the loathing of Hitler and his barbarous methods, is why America has always been so overwhelmingly anti-Nazi and anti-fascist.

America is fighting this war for her future and against the crippled future which Hitler planned for her. If Hitler had defeated Britain and Russia he would have turned his attention towards the western hemisphere. It is conceivable that he would not have attacked immediately. But the United States would not have trusted the chance. America would have prepared. America would have wanted the biggest air armada, the strongest army, the finest navy in the world. America would have become an armed camp. Americans would have lived like soldiers in a fortress ever on the alert against a sudden assault. The nation's economy would have been geared to defense year after year, year after year. Under such a strain, things happen to the political and social system, to the standard of living, and to nerves. Hitler took advantage of such conditions in France to weaken France before he struck.

That was the prospect before war was declared on America. It makes it clear that America was engaged in mortal combat with the Hitler corporation even before the bombs fell on Hawaii. Sooner or later, Hitler seeking world domination and the United States seeking to prevent it would have collided.

Two alternatives were open to the United States. One, to do nothing and wait until all anti-Hitler forces in the eastern hemisphere had been defeated and America had no potential allies; in that case, America might not have been attacked until Hitler had won the war and we stood alone. Or, two, to risk attack and help our allies while they were still standing so that we would not have to meet the victorious enemy alone. Under expert leadership and guided by the best intuition, America chose the second course.

Why did Japan attack the United States?

Japan could have taken the offensive against Siberia and then some Americans might have said, "We do not want to go to war to save Soviet Russia." Japan could have gone into Thailand and some Americans might have said, "Where's that?" and "Why is that any of our business?" Japan might have tried to seize the Dutch East Indies and offset the effect of America's economic boycott. Why did Japan make a frontal attack on the United States and thus make sure of America's immediate and full participation in the war?

In the last seven months of 1941, the Axis deliberately brought the two great non-belligerents, Russia and America, into the war by direct, unprovoked attacks. Russia was neutral. She was not about to strike Germany. Yet Hitler invaded Russia. The United States had no intention of attacking Japan. Yet Japan attacked the United States. Why? Why did Germany and Japan, of their own accord, drag two powerful countries like Russia and America into the war against them? The answer to this question is the key to the strategy of the war.

When it looked like victory for Hitler in Europe, in 1939 and 1940, the Japanese were not interested in entering the big war. Italy went into the war in June, 1940, because she thought it was over and wanted to make sure of a share in the loot. As somebody has said, "Mussolini gallantly rushed to the aid of the victor." (He has been slightly disappointed.) But the Japanese situation was different. They had a war of their own in China. Japan reckoned that a Hitler victory over the British would be a Japanese victory too, and Japan would gain many advantages in Asia without fighting. But in December, 1941, Germany was not winning as fast as Tokio had expected. America was coming into closer association with the anti-Axis powers. The U. S. Navy was already at war. American materials were moving in broader and faster streams to England and Russia. The United States was actually in the war but in such a way that the whole advantage was with the democracies. The mammoth weight of America was being thrown more and more into the balance against the Axis International. Hitler had invaded Russia because he could not invade England and wanted to make sure of a stalemate at best. Now Russia had stopped him. England was becoming stronger. America was doing more. Even the stalemate seemed threatened. The unique historic opportunity which the fascist countries thought they had to achieve world supremacy was slipping out of their fingers. This concerned Japan as much as Germany. Japan was not pulling Nazi chestnuts out of the fire. There were Japanese chestnuts in the same fire. Japan had dreamed of a "Co-Prosperity Sphere" in Asia which she would rule. That dream would vanish if Germany were defeated. Japan stepped in to prevent Germany's defeat and her own defeat. Japan cannot possibly hope to keep her gains in the Pacific if Germany is crushed and America and England emerge victorious.

It would have been bad Axis strategy to let America remain the unmolested arsenal of democracy and fight Germany at sea while Japan, the biggest untapped reserve of the Axis, remained passive. Some Anglo-American pressure had to be withdrawn from Germany in Europe and the Atlantic. Japan had to place herself in the scale opposite America so as to redress the balance between the fascist and democratic alliances.

Thus, Germany attacked Russia to win a draw. That purpose frustrated by Russia's gallant fight, Japan attacked America to win a draw for the Axis. Japan's conception was: to squeeze every advantage out of a surprise attack on America, Britain and the Dutch Empire; to ring the Japanese archipelago with a circle of outposts—the Philippines, Hong Kong, some Dutch islands, Singapore—and make Japan impregnable so that no fleet would dare to come near enough to assail her and no bombers could regularly bomb her; Japan might then collaborate with Hitler against Russia or invade India. If the solid Eurasian continent were brought under Aryan-Mongol control, the Axis could withstand a long siege. Japan's attack on America, in other words, was a daring bid for a protracted war in which the exhaustion of both sides and the inability of either side to get at the other would offer the best escape from a complete Axis defeat. It was a desperate attempt of the Fascist International to prevent a democratic victory.

In the first year of the war, Hitler almost won. It was dark night for the civilized world. In the second year of the war, despite many smashing Axis victories, the fascists were fought to a standstill. In the third year of the war, in the autumn of 1941, the faint dawn of victory appeared. In 1942, the democratic dawn grew brighter.

The democracies still have to win the war. They will yet lose many battles. But now that the war has become truly world-wide, and all the assets of the Hitler International, with the possible exception of a few small nations, have been invested in the struggle, it is clear that the Axis cannot win. Its greatest ambition is to stave off defeat. Military superiority is within the reach of the anti-Axis forces. They have to extend themselves to reach it. That is the difficult uphill task which lies ahead.

America, from now on, will play a decisive part in

this war. Later, when the United States is fully mobilized and producing at top capacity, America will play the major role in the victory. After the victory, America will be a primary factor in the peace.

Because of our strength and because of Britain's increasing dependence on us, America is first in war and will be first in peace. The war cannot be won without us and no peace can be stable or good without us.

Before the war, America was ambling along genially towards world leadership. This war is forcing America quickly to assume that leadership.

America can help lead mankind back to sanity and health. Then she can help wipe out want, war, economic insecurity, political insecurity, religious persecution, racial discrimination, and inequality of social and economic opportunity. The war was not started to achieve these things. But it could become the starting point for achieving them.

America's leadership in world affairs will give her tremendous power for good. She could make friends everywhere if she were not tempted to build a great empire or to forget that small countries and defeated peoples can be very proud and sensitive. The world will accept leadership. It will agree to form a big family striving together towards the better life. It will not long tolerate domination. The difference between world domination and world leadership is as big as the difference between war and peace. Domination is what Hitler wants. Domination is war. Enlightened leadership means peace.

But first the war must be won.

THE STRATEGY OF VICTORY

9. THE STRATEGY OF VICTORY

"I DON'T know," Winston Churchill replied when he was asked at a conference of British editors in the summer of 1941 how England could win the war.

"I don't know," Leopold S. Amery, Secretary of State for India, said to me when I asked him in 1941 how Great Britain could achieve victory. "But listen," he added. "In July, 1918, I was summoned to Prime Minister Lloyd George. The French and Italian governments, he said, had informed us that if the imminent Allied offensive in France failed as so many similar offensives had failed, they would retire from the war. Lloyd George accordingly instructed me to draw up a plan for the evacuation of the British army from the continent—a super-Dunkirk." That would have meant a German victory.

"You know what happened," Amery continued. "The July, 1918, offensive started and less than four months later we had won the war. Nobody ever asked me for my evacuation plan, and all that remains of it is my twelve pages of scribbled pencil notes. If you had asked me in July, 1918, how we were going to win the war I would have answered as I do now: 'I don't know.' Yet we won."

I was in France on September 3, 1939, when the second world war broke out. I encountered numerous

Frenchmen who were sure France would be defeated and who were panicky before the first shot was fired. But I have never met an Englishman who was not completely confident in victory. "We just can't lose" is the British refrain.

This faith is the foundation stone of victory.

But psychology alone does not win wars. The British belief in invincibility is based on the military successes recorded in their history—matched by no comparable defeats, on trust in the RAF, the Navy, Churchill, and the people, and on the expectation of American aid and continued Russian resistance. But with all their fortitude and determination, the British could not outline a strategy of victory because their limited strength did not allow them to seize the initiative. The initiative belonged to Hitler. Here and there in Libya, in the air and at sea, the British had occasionally gone forth to challenge the enemy, but by and large they had remained on the defensive, and in defense the outlines of the strategy of victory are very faint.

I was astounded to learn in London that after Dunkirk, in May, 1940, when the British hastily abandoned the European continent leaving most of their equipment behind them, the British army in England did not have even one fully equipped division. England was defended by fewer than 12,000 regular soldiers. A London friend said to me, "When we win the war and capture Hitler, we won't torture him. But we'll put him on an isolated isle as we did with Napoleon, and every morning we will read to him a list of the things we did not have in the summer of 1940 when he could have come in and smashed us."

The British still wonder why Hitler failed to invade them in July, 1940. The probable answer is that the German war on France was more of a campaign than its brief duration would suggest. The Germans captured more than two million prisoners and had to move most of them into Germany. The Vichy government has stated that in the short weeks of the Nazi war 266,805 French homes were bombed or shelled and 200,000 of these were destroyed. A total of 5,731 villages were hit by the war and of these 191 were more than half demolished. The Nazi invasion, Vichy's official report declared, caused more physical damage than any one year of the first world war. After that, Hitler had to do considerable "mopping up" in France, and then he had to clean up and regroup his forces and he overconfidently did that so slowly that when he started in August to prepare the invasion by a series of heavy air blitzes against England he soon discovered that he had missed his best chance; the RAF was too strong. That was Hitler's crowning military error.

British war industries are slow, and it took the British a very long time to replenish their stocks of arms after Dunkirk. A year later they were still inadequately supplied. In the autumn of 1941, Communists and others in Britain demanded a British offensive in western Europe to relieve German pressure on Russia. The demand came with bad grace from persons who, earlier, had lauded Stalin as a genius because he refrained from relieving German pressure on France and England. But when Russia was attacked they argued that Britain ought to take advantage of the preoccupation of an estimated eighty-five per cent of Hitler's armed forces in Russia by staging an offensive in France, Norway, Holland, Italy, or Spain. I discussed this question with several members of the British government and they gave a convincing answer: England simply lacked the arms and the ships for such action.

At that time, the British government was making accumulations of arms in Egypt for the Libyan offensive. Occasionally, and without much publicity, British units made quick-stab, hit-and-run raids on the continent in order to destroy property or take a few prisoners who could give information. One of the largest of these sorties was staged in the harbor of Narvik against the Lofoten Islands which Churchill called Lots of Fun. London would have liked to do more, but could not.

I asked a member of the British War Cabinet why 20,000 British soldiers could not be landed at Cherbourg, France.

"Suppose we did," he replied. "What good would it do?"

"Wouldn't it force Hitler to move some men from Russia?" I said.

"No," he answered. "He would let us stay there until he was ready to deal with us. He might bomb us. But we would not be able to disturb him very much."

"Couldn't you arm the French and start revolts?" said I, trying out on him arguments I had heard in favor of such action.

"Not now," he countered. "Not with the Gestapo

and German army as strong as they are today in France. We may do something elsewhere. But we cannot yet face the Germans on the European continent."

"Do you feel the same way about landing 200,000 British soldiers in Europe?" I persisted.

"Yes, only more so," he said. So much shipping would be required to move and supply such an army, he explained, and so many vessels would have to wait in idleness on the chance that the force might have to be hurriedly evacuated, that England would lose many valued cargoes from America on which subsequent strategy depended. Besides, England may not have had 200,000 armored troops in the second half of 1941.

So Britain remained on the defensive in Europe and Asia. But now the United States is in the war. The Red Army has given convincing proof of its prowess. The Dutch Empire fights well. China fights on. The British Empire is mobilized. It is time to plan the strategy of victory through offensive action. No war can be won on the defensive unless the enemy collapses from within.

What likelihood exists of political revolutions or economic paralysis in the Axis countries?

The Fascist system consists of the three suns: Germany, Japan, and Italy; a chain of stars: Hungary, Rumania, Bulgaria, Finland, Spain, and Thailand, which are held in position by the magnetism of the suns; and a host of moons—the conquered countries—where life is officially extinct except in the volcanoes. Of late, however, astrologers have noticed a strange phenomenon: Italy is being transformed into a moon. The weakest fascist sun is fast burning itself out.

Italy was exhausted by what for her were two major wars, those in Abyssinia and Spain, and by nineteen years of fascism. Then she entered this war. The Italian army and air force suffered heavy losses in Greece, Yugoslavia, Abyssinia, and Libya. Many of Mussolini's proud ships are at the bottom of the Mediterranean Sea. I think it is safe to say that if Italy had stood alone in this war she would already have been conquered by the democracies. But since she stands with Germany she has been conquered by Germany instead. As Mussolini's power in Italy recedes, that of Hitler advances. Nazi control is growing over the Italian armed forces, the Italian police, and Italy's economy. Italy is as much a vassal state as Czechoslovakia. Mussolini, who cannot fight his own battles, certainly had no desire to fight Hitler's in Russia. But he had to. On paper, it was to document "Europe's solidarity against Bolshevism." Actually, it was because Hitler ordered it.

Many Italians resent the German conquest of their country, and they increasingly resent Mussolini, whose ambitions and folly make him the architect of that humiliating enslavement. But they can do nothing about it. They cannot revolt against the combined forces of the Ovra, their own secret police, and the Gestapo, the imported Nazi secret police. The supplies of food, fuel, gasoline, and clothing in Italy are deficient and constantly shrinking. No toilet soap was available in Italy during the second half of 1941, the Italian government admits. Rome announces officially that the butter ration for 1942 is 2.45 ounces per month for each person. The bread ration is down to seven ounces a day. The sugar ration has been fixed at one pound a month, macaroni at two pounds a month. In these circumstances, Italy has no enthusiasm for the war which, for them, has become somebody else's war. But they are bound in strong chains. Even if Mussolini wished to take his country out of the war, the Germans would not let him. And the hope of retrieving his fortunes and reputation by an Axis victory holds him as firmly as the physical presence of the Germans. If Germany is defeated, Mussolini and fascism are finished in Italy. So Mussolini ignominiously drags along and serves his Berlin master.

Italy is nevertheless an asset to Hitler. She engages considerable anti-Axis armed forces; she has labor, industries, and ships which can work for Germany, and food which can be stolen for Germany. But as time goes on and as the British administer additional blows at Hitler's cringing ally, the law of diminishing returns begins to operate, and Italy leans more heavily on Germany while Germany gets less benefit out of Italy.

If Italy could be knocked out it would be a mortal setback for Hitler. He will therefore fight for Italy as he would for German soil. The fate of Italy depends, accordingly, on what happens in Nazi Germany.

In judging German domestic conditions and Hitler's prospects, we should not try to see the situation as we would like it to be but as it is. The outside observer must guard against exaggerations. Wishful thinking is dangerous because it is dangerous to underestimate the enemy. The best guides are statements from Nazi sources and incontrovertible objective facts.

The most significant and most revealing Nazi document on the war is the article, which I have already mentioned, by Dr. Goebbels, Nazi Propaganda Minister, first published in the Berlin weekly *Das Reich* and reprinted in full in the *New York Times* of November 10, 1941. The little doctor with the big mouth begins by attempting to justify Germany's precipitation of the war. "When you know you are facing a pitiless adversary," he says, "who is aiming a rifle toward you to fire from his most favorable position, the best policy is to anticipate his shots." These words, clearly, are Goebbels' answer to widespread feelings in Germany that Germany need not have gone to war, that nobody was attacking her. No, replies Goebbels, but someone would have attacked us. Anyway, he continues, "You are now involved in this struggle whether you want to be or not. Having begun to march we must march on. There is no longer a chance of withdrawing for any one of us." Apparently, Germans were arguing that it might be wise to stop or quit, and Goebbels' sensitive listening devices had caught this popular mood. The Nazi campaign in Russia was going badly at the time. "From the historic viewpoint," he philosophizes, "each individual campaign in this war amounts to a war in itself. If we do not wage it today we will in the future have to wage it under probably much more unfavorable conditions and circumstances." The apologetic tone is used throughout the article.

"Fate deals hard and relentlessly with us," he admits, "but it means well with us."

Yes, but when will it all be over, Germans have been asking. "More important than the question of when this war will end is how it will end," Goebbels replies. "If we win, all is won: raw materials, freedom, nourishment, Lebensraum, the basis for social reform of our state and the opportunity of full development for the Axis powers. If we lose, all this, this and still more, will be lost, namely our whole national existence."

Here Dr. Goebbels is trying to frighten the Germans. We will be crushed if we lose, he warns. A few months earlier, Goebbels had been painting for the German nation glorious pictures of the future in victory. Now he seeks to frighten them with the gloomy prospect of defeat. No leader speaks to his country that way if he thinks victory is soon to come. The Nazi appeal used to be: We shall win. Today it is: We dare not lose.

"The Axis powers," Goebbels continues, "actually are fighting for the most elemental existence, and the cares and burdens that must be laid on your shoulders in this war would pale before the inferno that awaits us should we lose the war." And on the same theme, "We know only too well what heavy sacrifices war demands of all of us. But are not the sacrifices of defeated nations, even if they now are living outside the pale of war, incomparably greater than ours?" This is a contemptible reference to France and the other Nazi-occupied countries. The Nazis first make conditions in those countries very bad and then point to them as examples of what Germany should try to avoid.

Throughout this remarkable article, one hears Goebbels answering murmurers and objectors. "Even though we are called upon to bear greater portions of the burdens of war, we are nevertheless among all European nations enjoying the highest standard of living. Certainly, we must put up with curtailments in many directions, but they are not by far as burdensome as to make them unbearable."

The doctor then launches into a hortatory peroration, and concludes, "Let us not ask: when will victory come, but instead see to it that it does come." Germans have obviously been asking when will victory come; otherwise Goebbels would not have told them not to ask.

Goebbels, to be sure, promises that in the end they will win. But his own words prove that his German readers are skeptical, cynical, and tired. Every foreigner who has been in Germany reports that none of Hitler's many mighty victories in the Lowlands, France, the Balkans, and Russia released enthusiasm or joy among the German people. The Germans remember, or were told, that between 1914 and 1918 Germany also won all the battles and then lost the war. That is why the Germans are not interested in victories but in victory which will end the war they hate so much. As the victories pile up they notice that the final victory eludes them, and it is final victory they want because it will herald the end of their acute wartime sufferings.

The nation least convinced of Germany's invincibility is the German nation. In the beginning they believed they would triumph quickly. Now they are losing faith. Two motives may inspire a country in war: the hope of winning or the fear of losing. Goebbels, suspecting with his keen perception that popular hope in victory was waning, seeks to stimulate the fear of defeat. He tells the nation what awaits them if the enemy triumphs: "If they succeed in overcoming us Germany will be destroyed, exterminated and extinguished. We cannot expect even a Versailles." That is not all. "One school" of thought in democratic countries, Goebbels informs those who read his article, "pleads for the dissolution of the unity of our defense system and our economic system, another for the regional decimation of our fabric of States, a third for birth control and reduction of our populations, and a fourth for sterilization of our entire population under sixty years." This throws light on the fascist's mentality; they can only see the enemy in their own image.

When Goebbels wrote this article to combat the mood of depression in Germany, Russia had not yet pushed the Nazi army back from Moscow. Since then, German troops have tasted defeat, for the first time, in Russia and in Africa. That further undermines the legend of invincibility. Hitler's failure to take Moscow before the winter, underlined by his curt dismissal of commander-in-chief General Walther von Brauchitsch, was a staggering blow to the German's belief in victory, as well as to the German's faith in Hitler, for Hitler had promised the fall of Moscow; he had always kept such promises; in this momentous instance he did not. And now America, to boot, has pitted its strength against the Axis world.

"I was at the front on that day in April, 1917, when the United States declared war on us," a German said to me on the day I first saw Berlin in December, 1921, "and I knew we had lost the war." America's reputation as a powerful industrial country has spread much further than in 1917. Not only Germany but all the world knows that in this mechanized war, American output will weight the balance heavily against the fascist constellation. Morale in Germany, bad before America's entry into the conflict, is worse now. Even when one is building a fence or planting a garden, confidence in the result acts as a spur. When millions of human lives are being invested and a whole nation is being ground in a merciless war machine it is rather depressing to have a gnawing suspicion that the entire effort is useless.

Germany has actually been at war since 1934. Ever since that year Germans have had to tighten their belts and strain their muscles and nerves to prepare for this war. The human animal is a marvelous contrivance and can stand a great deal. Modern history shows that. But there comes a time when the body and mind begin to weaken.

Experts in London have stated that the food situation in Germany is not disastrous. Hitler is gathering food in conquered countries and giving it to Germans. There are acute shortages of fats. Soap is scarce. British prisoners in Germany write home saying that they use the soap in the parcels which they get through the International Red Cross to obtain cigarettes, still available in adequate quantities in Germany, and other desirable objects.

The clothing situation in Germany is very unsatisfactory. The clothing ration, originally far below the British level which is just about satisfactory, was reduced forty per cent in the autumn of 1941. The British Ministry of Economic Warfare declares that German-controlled Europe produces only nine per cent of the cotton which Germany alone requires and only fifty-nine per cent of the wool. So that if Germany seized every shred of cotton and wool grown in Europe there would still be a serious shortage. Synthetic substitutes do not keep people warm; they are not durable and their manufacture makes heavy inroads on an already severely limited labor market. Not even the German army is furnished with warm clothing; on December 20, 1941, Hitler and Goebbels made a frantic public appeal to the population to give their winter clothing for the use of the Nazi legions stuck in Russia. "As long as a single object of winter clothing remains in the Fatherland," Goebbels commanded, "it must go to the front. I know," he added, "that also in the homeland the individual can spare such equipment only with great difficulty. He is not in a position to replace it. But a thousand times more urgently do our soldiers need such equipment which they cannot replace either."

A low spirit, cold, and just barely enough food along with very hard work over a prolonged period add up to susceptibility to illness and to reduced productive capacity. The deterioration is slow and imperceptible but constant. The British blockade contributes to it. I had several conversations in London with Dr. Hugh Dalton, Minister of Economic Warfare, the official in charge of the blockade. Could the blockade force Germany to her knees? There was no way of telling. It plays its part in wearing out the enemy. Any definite calculation depends on how much fighting Germany is doing, what territories she has conquered, what she gets out of them, who are her unconquered friends, what she can produce in the form of substitutes—oil, rubber, wool, and so forth—and what leaks in the naval cordon remain open. The invasion of Russia deprived Hitler of Russian supplies and of supplies which reached Germany through Vladivostok on the Pacific. The further west the British get in North Africa and the more completely the democratic fleets control the Mediterranean and the Atlantic the less the leakage. Dr. Dalton offered the view that the blockade shortened the first world war by six months. There can, naturally, be no complete analogy between any two complicated situations and certainly not between the first and second world wars. At best, the blockade hampers and embarrasses Germany's war effort and forces her to extend her fighting lines by invading countries against the dictates of military strategy.

Even in normal peace times, Europe never had enough food to feed itself or enough raw materials to keep itself employed. In 1918, Germany and her allies controlled about as much territory as they do now. She did not have France or Italy or Norway, but she had the Caucasus and the oil of Baku and access to the Turkish empire in Asia and vast unscorched lands in Russia. Moreover, that war did not consume so much raw material. And Germany was not being bombed. Yet she went down to defeat. Japan, in 1918, was in the democratic camp. Now it is with Hitler. But Russia, in 1918, had had a revolution and was out of the war. Now it is a dagger in Hitler's side.

Ah, yes, cries Goebbels who knows that Germans are thinking about 1918, but you must not draw false comparisons! At that time, he says, "it was the leaders of Germany, not the people, who proved unequal to the task."

This is an adored Nazi myth. Hitler used it to build his popular following. He said the leaders in Berlin betrayed the nation in 1918 and Jews, Socialists, and pacifists stabbed the army in the back. But, as usual, the Nazis ignore the facts of history. On August 8, 1918, General Ludendorff, Germany's greatest military genius, wrote, "The war must be ended." On September 29, 1918, the German General Staff clamored for an armistice, and General Hindenburg declared, "The military situation admits of no delay." The Kaiser's army lost the war even though it still stood on foreign soil. But this was not a purely military development. The army reacted to the mood of the people, among whom undernourishment, which commenced in earnest in 1917, fatigue, and the depression resulting from the defection of Turkey and Bulgaria caused deep discontent. There followed revolts, mutinies, and the final collapse. Not only did the leaders prove inadequate to the task in 1918, but also the army and the people. That is the record. It could happen again. Friction between Hitler and his generals, and between Hitler and his party henchmen, reflects the increasing tension. Hitler is a stabilizing factor by reason of his tremendous psychological hold on many Germans, particularly women. If he dies or is killed or eats too much carpet and loses his working capacity, Germany's fighting ability would be appreciably reduced.

It is very important that the Nazis are psychologically on the defensive. German Foreign Minister Joachim von Ribbentrop said on December 23, 1941, that Nazi soldiers were fighting to prevent "a pitiless adversary from wiping out their women, their children, their country—their whole people." This would be a strong rallying cry if the people believed it and cared. Perhaps the Nazis have deliberately adopted the new Cassandra propaganda line to arouse the nation from the lethargy induced by sterile victories. But it smacks of defeatism, and by its contrasts with earlier prophecies of triumph it emphasizes the sad turn of the German wheel of fortune.

Germany's sudden collapse from within is always a possibility. If it comes, all the better. But it should not enter into the calculation of the foes of the Axis. In a dictatorship, fear of the murderous and ubiquitous secret police paralyzes most subversive activity and keeps the lid pressed down on embryonic popular protests. Opposition exists. Protestant and Catholic churchmen inside Germany have bravely voiced it before their congregations. In London I saw the full texts of some of their sermons which were smuggled out of Germany. Remnants of old political parties conduct sporadic underground propaganda activity. But Germany will have to suffer many more military reverses before domestic unrest begins to pull down the Nazi structure. The effectiveness of foreign anti-Nazi propaganda, when intelligent, is also in direct ratio to the number of Nazi military setbacks and to the length of the war.

The key to Germany's morale, and Japan's morale as well, is offensive military action by the anti-fascist forces.

In reckoning the striking power that remains in the Nazi regime, the Nazi-occupied countries figure both as liabilities and assets. However, the assets are real and the liabilities are more potential than real. The Nazi-dominated lands are liabilities to the extent that they are unwillingly dominated and have to be policed. They create a feeling of uncertainty in Germany about the future. The Nazi conquerors are not liked in any country they control. The fawning Quislings among the natives are not liked. This is proved by the numerous officially announced arrests which the Germans make in all the seized territories, and the frequent execution of hostages and the many fines imposed. The whole continent of Europe is seething, and it gives the Germans an uncomfortable sense of sitting on the lid of a boiling caldron. Reliable reports reach London of bribe-taking and other forms of corruption among German officers and German officials in occupied countries. This adds to Nazi demoralization. Germans in the armies of occupation admit that their throats will be slit if Germany loses the war. They know they are hated.

Every month an average of one hundred Norwegians cross the stormy North Sea in fishing boats and sailboats to enlist in the British Navy in Scotland. Poles come halfway across the globe and turn up in Britain or British possessions to join the anti-Axis armed forces. In Czechoslovakia there is a far-flung, smoothly functioning organization, which enjoys the help of anti-Nazi Germans high in the Nazi service of that country and which supplies the British with some of their best information about Hitler politics. British airmen who have to bail out over Holland or France usually get back to England, through an underground system operated by the local inhabitants. British pilots have told me that when flying over Holland, Norway, and France they often get light signals from people on the ground to help them bomb the very areas where these people live. My Free French friends in London showed me handwritten letters regularly received in large numbers from occupied and unoccupied France. I read many of them. They usually begin with complaints about the bad food situation. "The old man," Marshal Pétain, they say, does the best he can in difficult circumstances but he cannot prevent France from being used as a tool by the Nazis. "The sailor," Admiral Darlan, is a Nazi stooge. "Why don't the British bomb us more?" several of the letters asked. "Our only hope of salvation is in a British victory." Some letters ended with the hope that the "censor will let me say this." On four letters

THE STRATEGY OF VICTORY 207

which I saw, the censor replied in his own handwriting, "Why not? I agree with you."

After I had spoken about these letters to one audience in America, a lady came up to me and said, "You told us these letters arrive in London from occupied and unoccupied France. I did not know there was anybody in unoccupied France." In varying degrees, both parts of France are occupied, occupied by the Germans. In Vichy sits Marshal Pétain, the hero of the great battle of Verdun in the first world war where hundreds of thousands of Frenchmen died and were wounded under German fire in order to fulfill the promise of "They Shall Not Pass." Now the Germans pass through Pétain's office every day. The French resent it all the more because they cannot help it.

The French leaders capitulated in June, 1940, not because they were defeated but because they thought that Britain would soon be defeated and the war would be over. Winston Churchill warned the French that England would fight on, even if left alone. But when Premier Reynaud passed that message on to Pétain and other French generals, they replied, "In three weeks, England will have her neck wrung like a chicken." The generals were sure England would fall, and they hoped to get better terms from Hitler by submitting earlier. But the continued resistance of the British and now of the Russians has made all the difference in France and in other occupied countries. They see a hope of throwing off the Nazi yoke. They wish to add their effort to this consummation. The longer the war lasts the less they believe in the permanence of their present defeat.

When the United States entered the war their faith in ultimate redemption grew even stronger. As time goes on, therefore, the occupied countries become bigger headaches to the Nazis. It costs Hitler more to keep order. The occupying regiments have to be moved more frequently lest they be contaminated by contact with the occupied. Sabotage in factories grows. Consequently Nazi repression grows. That adds fuel to the fire of the population's resentment.

Fed by intelligent propaganda about the future that awaits Europe after the war—for the Nazis assiduously preach the advantages of a unified Europe purged of the "pluto-democracies"—and by democratic victories, this fire could burn more brightly with each passing month and help light the road to victory.

Meanwhile, however, the occupied countries are growing food for Germany, making munitions for Germany and sending workingmen to Germany. They do it under compulsion; nevertheless, the Nazis benefit. In Germany, and in German-held countries, there are millions of eager anti-Nazis eager to make a contribution to Hitler's downfall. The infection will spread when the foes of the Axis move forward in battle. But Hitler remains a mighty enemy.

The same is true of Japan. Experts on Japan have stated for years that Nippon's economy is on the brink of disaster, and no doubt it is. Yet it could apparently stand on the brink for a long time. The living standard of Japan's population has been depressed to a very low minimum. The war in China, which began in 1931 and in earnest in 1937, has taxed the nation's resources and strength. Despite all that, Japan struck a mighty blow at America, Britain, and Holland when she went to war. Perhaps Japan is incapable of sustained effort and prolonged resistance. But there is not much sense in taking comfort from the mathematical inferiority of the enemy. It is possible to draw up two columns of figures, one giving the resources of the Axis powers, an opposite column showing the resources of the anti-Axis powers, and to prove that the whole thing is ridiculous: The Axis never had a chance; it might just as well give up now. But it continues to win battles, sink ships, and conquer territories.

The United States Census Bureau presents data on the comparative strengths of the two belligerent combinations. The anti-Axis group has 86% of the oil of the world; the Axis only 3%. The remaining 11% is where the Axis cannot get it. Coal: Axis 29%, anti-Axis 67%. Iron: Axis plus Sweden, which because of its geographic position works only for Germany—that is why Hitler has not yet attacked it—27%, anti-Axis 64%. Wheat: Axis 21%, anti-Axis 69%.

The area of the anti-Axis league is thirteen times as great as that of the Axis countries. The population of the British Empire, the United States, China, Russia, the Dutch Empire, and the friendly Latin American nations equals 1,469,647,000 against 521,505,000 in Germany, Italy, Japan, the occupied countries of Europe, and Indo-China and Thailand in Asia. Counting only men between 18 and 35, men who can become good soldiers, the United States alone has 22,796,000 compared to 28,560,000 in Germany, Italy, and Japan. If China and India are included on the anti-Axis side, the fighting man-power reserves are 163,887,000 against only 28,560,000 for the fascist enemy. The United States Steel Institute announces that for every two tons of steel which can be manufactured in all the Axis and Axis-dominated nations combined, the United States can make three tons. At the end of 1942, the United States will have a steel-producing capacity of 88,000,000 tons; Japan only 7,100,000 tons.

These facts are encouraging. They are the basis of the widespread conviction that Hitler and his satellites cannot win this war. But when one remembers how many crushing defeats the Axis forces have inflicted on their enemies it becomes clear that the thing which matters most is not what you have but what you do with it. Men do not affect the outcome of the war unless they are trained fighters or are making munitions or are otherwise directly engaged in the war effort. Industrial capacity is not contributing to victory if it is employed in the production of vacuum cleaners. We must stop counting what the enemy does not have and start making what we have count.

The first element in the strategy of victory is the conversion of our resources into fighting units, equipped with all the apparatus of attack and defense, and transported to a point of contact with the enemy.

In England and in America the inhabitants are still living too well for wartime. If human life is conscripted, and nothing is holier, then even property must be subject to conscription. If men are ready to give up their lives and if women are ready to give up their men so as to win a war that must be won, then everybody should be ready to give up the luxuries and comforts whose production will interfere with the production of weapons. When we use what we already own there can be no objection unless the armed forces need those facilities. But if we consume materials or labor which could be of greater benefit to the armed services we are, to that extent, obstructing the successful operation of the war. This is the criterion which has been applied in Germany, Russia, Italy, and Japan. One usually does not wish to copy the social or political methods of these countries, but in the mobilization of war assets we can learn from them. The less intensive our war effort the more extensive the war will be.

America's industry, geared to high action, can outproduce all the enemy nations. Before we went to war, President Roosevelt proclaimed the United States "the arsenal of democracy." We are still the arsenal of democracy and of Russia when it is fighting democracy's foes. China, Russia, the Dutch Empire, and Britain and the Dominions need American supplies. If Russia is facing the bulk of the Nazi army, she is more entitled to American munitions than United States units not in the front line of battle. Priorities should be determined by an enlightened selfishness.

All the munitions output of the anti-Axis nations must be entered into a single ledger and disposed of according to need. The production of those munitions ought to be co-ordinated so that an American gun brought to the Pacific area could fire shells made in Australia, and so that a South African motor would fit into a California-made bomber. Nations fighting together for their lives should share their industrial secrets and their economic information. That will advance the cause of practical internationalism. A factory which has invented a new machine or new method for producing munitions hastens the democratic victory by passing on the invention to its domestic business competitors as well as to foreign firms making the same equipment for use against the same enemy. The government should be authorized to redistribute workingmen, engineers, raw materials, and plant facilities so that they do the greatest military good. Old customs, old thoughts, old institutions, old prejudices, and old fogies should be brushed aside, if necessary, to pave the way to victory. Waste and inefficiency in wartime kill young men. If inefficiency in England can be eliminated by American methods the British should be willing to forget their sensibilities and remember only the stakes in this war. Americans should be equally accessible to outside education. The co-ordination of the anti-Axis war effort should not begin in the General Staffs but in factories and industries and industrial-planning boards. What we need is an Industrial General Staff for all democratic countries. The experience gathered by it will be useful after the war.

An economic strategy of victory is the best, in fact the only, foundation of a military strategy of victory.

How, in the end, will the Axis countries be defeated if they do not fall apart from their own rottenness? The British put great faith in the bomber. Some of the most important men in England believe that if they could attain overwhelming air superiority they would be on the highway to ultimate success. "The bomber," says Sir Archibald Sinclair, Secretary of State for Air, "is a weapon which, if properly used with ruthless efficiency, can ruin Hitler's hopes." He avoids exaggeration. "Our bombers are laying siege to the entire German military machine. It will be a long and hard siege. The German machine is enormous, organized over a period of years with German thoroughness, and defended on a vast scale. The damage we are doing is not yet apparent in any slackening of the German military effort. The walls still stand and the roof still glitters, but it is the foundations we are undermining."

In addition to this cryptic statement, however, Sir Archibald once said in a Newcastle speech that England aims "to bring the Germans to their knees by the mightiest air attack ever envisaged."

The question immediately arises how the British could bring the Germans to their knees with bombs when the Germans failed to achieve the same end by air-raiding Britain. "Our pilots are better," was one answer given me by a member of the British War Cabinet. "Their aim and navigation are better." He explained that Nazi airmen had been trained originally on the assumption that Britain would be subdued in mass daylight attacks and they were therefore taught to follow the squadron- or wing-leader. "The Germans are inferior when on their own." The Germans expected the war to be short. The British planned, from the very beginning, for a long war. "We started by making few machines but good ones. Every boy in the RAF feels, when he goes aloft, that he is king of the air. He is thoroughly trained. He has confidence in his machine."

There is a considerable measure of truth in these British boasts. Moreover, the average German bomb dropped on Britain in the big blitzes weighed five hundred pounds, whereas the average British bomb now weighs two thousand pounds. A flying officer said to me in London, "I hope the Jerries don't discover the secret of the new explosive we have been putting into our bombs." British missiles have a terrible effectiveness.

Several persons, quite unconnected, told me in England that Great Britain was now reaping the fruits of the Nazi terror against scientists. Many of these scientists, some German, some Jews, some Czechs, are now working in British laboratories, and their labors have enhanced the power of British weapons of war. Contrariwise, the large-scale enforced exodus of scientific brains from Germany beginning with the advent of Hitler in 1933 is beginning to tell on the Nazi war machine.

These factors operate in favor of the British. But there are countervailing disadvantages. The first is Germany's anti-aircraft guns. The city of Berlin alone is protected by more anti-aircraft guns than all of Britain, and every RAF airman who has flown over Berlin, and over many other German cities, knows the murderous barrage those guns can throw into the air. The second disadvantage is geography. The Germans, with aerodromes in Holland and France, have only a short distance to fly to Britain, whereas the British must traverse hundreds of miles before they reach the main centers of German population and production. The geographic relation between England and Germany for purposes of air warfare has been compared to that of a tall lean man dancing with a fat lady. She is always nearer to him than he is to her.

All these handicaps can be overcome, the British argue, by faster and bigger bombers in vastly increased numbers. The German Luftwaffe's worst raid on England was launched on May 10, 1941. Fewer than one thousand bombers participated. British officials told me that thirty consecutive days of such raids would have paralyzed England. The Germans lost too many planes in that raid and their air force was too weak to continue the attacks. The size of the German air force has always been exaggerated. It was exaggerated by Lindbergh after his visits to Germany, and, after him, by others. The fact is that while the Luftwaffe was engaged in Russia it did not have enough surplus striking power to launch one single serious air raid upon Britain. The German air force is no longer the terrifying psychological deterrent it used to be.

With enough powerful planes, therefore, the RAF could hasten Germany's defeat. It is the view of many cautious experts that if and when Germany could be raided by three thousand bombers every day for sixty days, the Nazi war machine would be seriously crippled.

This task requires between forty and fifty thousand bombers. It cannot be undertaken, therefore, before

1943. Let us assume that on May 1, 1943, the RAF has 25,000 bombers, enough crews to man them and enough airfields from which to launch them. The preparations are already under way. Some of the bombers and some of the crews will be American. Every day in May, three thousand machines raid Germany. Assume that an average of six hundred planes are lost each day. On June 1, the RAF would have seven thousand planes left. During May, however, the RAF would have received from American and British factories eighteen thousand additional planes. It would also have sufficient reserve pilots recruited at home and abroad and in the empire. It would, accordingly, start June with 25,000 bombers and continue bombing Germany with three thousand bombers per day. At the end of those sixty days of incessant bombing of her factories, railways, roads, airports, and cities, Germany would be so "softened" as to put victory within the reach of the anti-Axis powers. The key to air warfare is: No interruption. The enemy must not be given the opportunity to repair damage or resume production or move food and other supplies or to sleep or to rest their nerves. In May and June, 1943, the Germans will be more fatigued and disgruntled by the prolongation of the war than they are today, and in greater despair. Giant air raids at such a juncture might produce national panic and a mood of surrender, and inflict decisive material damage.

Will England and America have fifty thousand bombers in the middle of 1943 to devote to a majestic if cruel assault on the German citadel? President Roosevelt told

THE STRATEGY OF VICTORY

Congress on January 6, 1942, that he had ordered American industry to produce forty-five thousand combat planes in 1942 and one hundred thousand combat planes in 1943. This is an "industrial miracle." Some of these machines will not be bombers. Some will be lost in the fighting before the great offensive in the summer of 1943. But with Britain's output, the united nations could have fifty thousand bombers, or even more, to assail Germany. The secret of victory is in the factories of America and England.

But not alone in the factories. Sixty days of unprecedentedly large air raids on Germany must be followed by a democratic invasion of the European continent at several points where anti-Axis naval and air supremacy could overcome Nazi resistance on the coast. Such landings, staged at places as far apart as Norway and Spain, France, Greece and Italy would divide Germany's armed forces and give the democrats numerous initial strategic advantages.

The Nazi blitzkrieg in Scandinavia, France, and the Balkans has left a profound impression on many minds. Even now it may seem unrealistic to plan to confront the German army on the battlefield. But the Reichswehr is no longer that perfectly polished, smoothly oiled mechanism which rolled over most of Europe. It has lost many of its best generals by death and "resignation." Hundreds of thousands of its finest troops are buried on the endless steppes of Russia. The Red Army, and the cold, checked Hitler's legions and drove them back from Moscow. The British defeated them in Libya. Time, the blockade, and bombs are not increasing the German army's power nor improving German morale. The heavy casualties in Russia have seriously depressed the German nation. If, in the summer of 1943, the democratic allies had two or three million well-trained, superbly equipped soldiers, eager for action and sure of victory, they could meet a tired, disspirited Reichswehr at a dozen Waterloos and win.

The fate of Germany is the key to the outcome of this war. For Italy would fall with Germany if she did not gracefully precede her big Nordic brother. And then Japan would be a lesser problem. Japan must be seriously resisted every day, everywhere. Nevertheless, and although Nazi Germany is a stronger country than Japan, it may take longer to defeat Japan than Germany because Japan is an island and by lightning offensives has seized so many outposts of that island archipelago that few battleships can approach Japan proper and few aeroplanes can regularly bomb her.

It would be much more difficult to get at the Japanese than at the Germans. England is a near base for Anglo-American air, naval, and land operations against Germany, and in certain circumstances Africa can serve the same purposes against Nazi-Europe. But the united nations hold no suitable base for an invasion of Japan.

Assuming that Russia will, with the aid of Anglo-American supplies which can reach the Red Army only through the very narrow transportation bottlenecks of Archangel and Iran, exact a further heavy toll of German casualties, the invasion of Europe is a more practicable expedient than the physical invasion of Japan.

This second world war cannot be won in the air alone. Blockade alone will not win it. Unless there is internal collapse in enemy countries, their defeat can only be administered by men on the ground. The prospect is not inviting. The undertaking is gigantic. An AEF in Europe is not at all the same proposition now as in 1917 and 1918 when the Atlantic was safer than it is today, when the aeroplane did not have the same terrors, and when France offered a welcome landing place and stable front for American troops. But the victor must take risks, make sacrifices and pay the high cost of victory. The democracies must attack.

Industrial and military preparations for democratic offensives require reinforcement from a third department—psychology. The ground for the democratic invasion of Europe is being prepared by Nazi repression, barbarism, and plunder in the conquered countries. But that is not enough. Before large numbers of citizens in those countries will risk their lives in "Fifth Column" co-operation with the invading democrats they must be sure of the fate that awaits them when the war is over. The European continent knows conservative England and does not always trust her. The European continent remembers the flamboyant promises made during the last war. Tragic experiences have bred a lot of skeptics in Europe. If the Greeks cast in their lot with invading democrats and help expel the Italians and Germans what regime will they get? Another fascist dictator like Metaxas, or democracy? Do the British and French favor a progressive republic in Spain, or the fascist Franco, or some other general? The people do the fighting and the people will ask searching questions. They will want to know what they are fighting for. They will examine the democracies bringing gifts. They will inquire whether the United States supports only democrats in the Western Hemisphere. They will wonder about democracy in the British Empire. They may suspect that the invading democrats will support undemocratic regimes in Europe. What about all the comings and goings of the Ottos and Carols? Europe must be purged of doubts about democracy before it is purged of the Nazis. For the Nazis have sowed many doubts in the minds of Europeans. They have exposed many of the weaknesses and hypocrisies of democratic governments. The European democracies were so full of flaws and injustices before 1939 that millions of people will hesitate to die in order to restore them.

Even in America and Britain, an increasing percentage of the population is passionately concerned with the shape of the peace to come. People say, "Of course we must win. But then what?"

THE SHAPE OF THE PEACE
TO COME

10. THE SHAPE OF THE PEACE TO COME

THERE could be a third world war.

The war of 1914-1918 was supposed to be a "war to end wars." We won it, but it failed to end wars. A war may be won and then lost in the peace that follows it. A war may also be lost while it is being won.

Realistically, the chief element in the next peace will be the attitude of the victorious nations towards the defeated nations. In England I therefore tried to find out what the British were thinking and feeling about Germans. Almost everybody told me that the British did not hate the Germans. There is much less hate for Germany in this war than in the last war. The hate is directed against "him," against Hitler. When there is an air raid, the English say, "'He' was over last night." Hitler and the Nazi "gangs of bandits," as Winston Churchill has called them, are blamed for Germany's crimes, not the German people. There would, accordingly, be no emotional barrier in Britain towards a sensible, liberal peace with the German people.

This is important, for if you erect such a barrier in war you may ruin the peace. The sentiments created and aroused during the present war will shape the peace.

In a very exact sense, therefore, the peace is being made every day of the war.

Storm Jameson wrote me a note during my stay in England in which she spoke of the Germans as "Boches." I chided her for the expression, and she wrote back, "Most Germans are Boches. Or at lease they will always be Boches for English of my generation and upbringing, though you wouldn't notice it if you listen to me talking to them after the war. I will be sensible and polite."

While only a very small minority of British people are emotionally anti-German—and I think this is equally true today of America—Englishmen are being subjected to propaganda which aims to make them intellectually anti-German. Lord Vansittart, former permanent chief of the British Foreign Office, is the leader of the school of thought which blames the German race, not the Nazis, for this war, for the last war, in fact, for most of the European wars of modern times. Vansittartism is a growing trend.

In his book, *Black Record*, and regularly in the Conservative *London Sunday Times*, Vansittart dissects German history and concludes that Frederick the Great and the Kaiser were only earlier Hitlers, and that the Germans are a "race of hooligans" and willing dupes of rapacious, militaristic conquerors. "Generations of us have never tasted *real* peace," he writes, "and we never will taste it until the incubus is removed." A "drastic" cure must therefore be administered to the German people which "will take at least a generation." "The soul" of Germany must be changed, Vansittart asserts. The victors must bring about the "regeneration of the Brazen Horde"—the German people.

In thus placing on Germany the sole guilt for many decades of European woes, Vansittart seems to be looking ahead to his kind of vindictive peace. But actually he is looking backward. Whatever Vansittart's personal motive, the implication of Germany's "black record" is that Britain's record is white. If Germany made all the wars, then the rest of us are innocent; nothing was wrong in England or France or America or Russia before this war; it was not Neville Chamberlain and the Conservative appeasers; it was not social evils—it was Germany. And so, after this war, all we have to do is to deal properly with Germany and we will have peace. By burdening Germany with all the blame for the world's ills the British Tories seek to absolve themselves and to counteract the tendency towards post-war reform in British domestic affairs and in international organization. The thesis would be: Only Germany is responsible for the war; Britain is not at fault; so why alter anything in the British economic, social, or political systems? Vansittartism is Conservative propaganda for the status quo which existed before the war. Neville Chamberlain was an appeaser largely because he feared that in a war the old England he loved would die and be succeeded by a new progressive England. But Churchill believes that the old English order can fight the war and win it and thereby win for itself the right to go on living. Churchill has repeatedly discouraged discussion of the peace.

When optimists plan for world reconstruction and

world federation their schemes are branded an "Escape to Utopia," and they are advised to win the war first. Meanwhile, however, the Tories are erecting bulwarks against a better kind of solidly organized peace by implying that all this is not necessary. "You merely have to put Germany in her place."

Lord Vansittart has read the Versailles Peace Treaty. It attributes the sole guilt for the first world war to Germany. But he has also read the secret diplomatic treaties and documents published by most of the foreign offices of Europe as well as their analyses by conscientious historians, and he knows they prove that the responsibility for the first world war was very widely distributed and shared, in varying degree, by all the great imperialist powers—Russia, Germany, Austria-Hungary, France, Italy, Turkey, Britain, and Japan. Their alliances were sordid bargains often contracted at the expense of helpless peoples (England with Russia, England and France with Italy in 1915, and so forth).

Fewer countries are directly culpable for the second world war. This war is the culmination and logical consequence of the fascist attacks on Manchuria, China, Abyssinia, Spain, Austria, and Czechoslovakia. Japan's aggression in Manchuria occurred in 1931 before Hitler was in office. Germany had nothing to do with it; Germany was a weak democracy at the time. Mussolini's invasion of Abyssinia took place when Italy was friendly with England and France, and hostile to Nazi Germany. Aggression, therefore, is not peculiarly Hitlerian or German. Nor is fascism or militarism uniquely

THE SHAPE OF THE PEACE TO COME 227

German. Italian fascism antedated the Hitler regime. Japanese militarism is a native product.

The evils of fascism, aggression, and dictatorship are not confined to one race or one country. We are faced with a far-flung social phenomenon which has deep, universal roots. The picture of the problem is blurred and the solution postponed by overemphasizing German racial characteristics. Conquering French armies once rolled over Europe just as conquering Nazi armies have done more recently. The British devoted their energies to overseas conquests. Admittedly, one race is not like the other, and the Germans do seem to enjoy discipline and marching. The Italians do not, yet they have been ruled by a ruthless autocrat. The Spaniards are mild and charitable, but Franco's dictatorship has been brutal and bloody. The Russians are kind and mellow; Stalin's regime is the opposite. The British have dropped bombs on defenseless villages in India. During the Syrian disturbances, the French behaved like Huns. Austria is the symbol of *Gemuetlichkeit*, of soft, easy-going charm. Yet the Austrian government fired cannon into workers' tenements in Vienna in 1934. No government anywhere has ever done such a thing. Cruelty recognizes few boundaries.

Nations sometimes get the governments they deserve. Often, however, they get worse than they deserve. To blame peoples for the deeds of the dictatorships which oppress them is to overlook the very nature of dictatorship, of government, and of modern propaganda. Hitler does not ask consent for his deeds. He acts first and then wins a semblance of popular approval by smashing opposition and subjecting the whole country to plausible, repetitive explanations and to emotional storms which the masses of any nation would resist with difficulty. A dictatorship is like a country permanently at war; the dictator seeks to establish an atmosphere of patriotic frenzy in which the critical faculty and the capacity to think begin to die. The people are helpless not merely because they dread the punishment of a ubiquitous secret police, but because they live in a constant climate of one-sided argument. My Soviet friends in Russia would frequently come to me to hear about the outside world and try to get a balanced view. The Kremlin discouraged such contacts between Russians and foreigners because it wanted its citizens to hear only the official versions of events. Fear and government monopoly of propaganda are every dictatorship's sharpest weapons; of these the latter is the more potent as far as the bulk of the population is concerned. Even when the public appears to sanction the dictator's misdeeds, therefore, the crime and guilt are primarily his. If all Germans are pro-Hitler why the concentration camps and the terror? Why the known opposition of church leaders and labor leaders?

A peace with retribution would make millions of innocents suffer with the guilty. It would also ignore the truth that Hitler, Mussolini, Stalin, the Tokio militarists, Franco, and other lesser totalitarians are not merely personal devils or expressions of national peculiarities but the products of vast world changes. The world has been sick. It was sick before Hitler. In fact, Hitler and the other dictators are symptoms of the dis-

THE SHAPE OF THE PEACE TO COME 229

ease. The dictatorships are a misconceived attempt to cure the disease. Hitler is a hurricane tearing at the foundations of modern society. If the structure had not been rotten he would not have succeeded in destroying so much of it. If democracy in Europe had been real, it would not have succumbed to Hitler and Mussolini. The defeat of Hitler, Mussolini, and Japan, therefore, is not enough. Having defeated them the world must defeat the conditions that made them. President Roosevelt, referring to the future peace, said in a fireside chat in June, 1941, "We will not accept a world like the post-war world of the 1920's, in which the seeds of Hitlerism can again be planted and allowed to grow." Our job is thus not the annihilation of Germans. We must build a new world with a climate which would not permit Hitlers to be born.

Hitler's New Order, though he seeks to fashion it with the tank, bayonet, and lash, is nevertheless based on the healthy idea that there must be a unified Europe without high national barriers obstructing sensible economic co-operation. The Roosevelt-Churchill Atlantic Charter, dated August 14, 1941, and adhered to by twenty-four additional governments on January 1, 1942, pledges the signatory powers "to endeavor, with due respect for their existing obligations, to further the enjoyment by all states, great and small, victor and vanquished, of access, on equal terms, to the trade and to the raw materials of the world which are needed for their economic prosperity." This describes something which has not been done before in the world; it has not even been attempted. World trade and the world's raw materials have hitherto not been equitably distributed. That is the cause of many of our troubles. The fascist states proposed to redistribute raw materials by seizing the wealth of their neighbors. But the problem is not solved by grabbing what others had previously grabbed. Such an attempt led to this war and would lead to endless wars. The redistribution should be by just and fair agreement; but redistribution there must be.

When the Atlantic Charter pledges that "victor or vanquished" will be included in this economic reform it recognizes that the defeated nations must be part of the peace and not only its victims. I cannot imagine how the victors could proceed if they decided to omit Germany, Italy, and Japan from future economic cures. The omission would vitiate the cure. As Foreign Secretary Eden declared on July 29, 1941, "A starving and bankrupt Germany in the midst of Europe would poison all of us who are her neighbors. That is not sentiment. It is common sense."

Point Eight of the Atlantic Charter provides that the aggressors of the past be disarmed as a preliminary to general disarmament. Several weeks after the Charter was framed I discussed it with ex-Prime Minister Lloyd George. Referring to its disarmament provision, he said with a smile and a twinkle in his blue eyes, "Eh, I think we had that in the Versailles Treaty." Germany was disarmed after Versailles; yet she rearmed. The only effective way of forcibly disarming Germany forever is to ruin her economically. If Germany is permitted to keep her chemical factories she can at some

THE SHAPE OF THE PEACE TO COME 231

later date manufacture powder and explosives. If she retains her steel mills she will be able to make tanks, guns, and shells. If she has shipbuilding facilities she can produce submarines.

A punitive peace cannot be a partially punitive peace. It must be complete. The defeated nations must be plowed up and sowed with thorns. Their populations must be removed. Otherwise the vanquished will rise again with bitter revenge in their hearts.

But the economic destruction of Germany, Italy, and Japan would destroy the destroyers too. The ruin of such big countries or even the retarding of their recovery would be a disaster to the victors. The experience of England and France after 1919 showed that it was not possible to collect reparations from Germany without first making Germany prosperous. Later, the world realized that German reparations payments were an embarrassment to those who received the money. It was America which really paid reparations for Germany. The large sums involved in reparations or in the war debts could simply not have been transferred without upsetting international finance. That is why almost all good British economists are now saying, No reparations. In other words, the retribution after this war cannot be economic. Therefore disarmament would be unreal, for the moment the victors stopped policing, the defeated countries could rebuild the industrial facilities for rearmament.

Nor is there a guarantee of peace in geographic adjustments. European security will not be achieved by snatching a piece of territory from one country and patching it on to another. Versailles did that in 1919. Shortly after the second world war started, Leslie Hore-Belisha, then British Secretary of State for War, said very aptly, "This is not a war about a map." Some shifting of boundaries will probably be unavoidable. Mere map-carving, however, cannot create the new Europe. Nor will the vivisection of Germany do it.

The basic idea of Versailles was to detach certain territories from Germany in order to make her weaker and then to surround her with a group of allies of France—Poland, Czechoslovakia, Rumania, Yugoslavia, and, in part, Italy—who would safeguard France against a German attack. But this system worked only while Germany was too weak to dispute it—which means that it never worked. A Versailles peace after the present war would be more difficult and less workable because the system that failed when applied to Germany alone would have to be applied to Germany, Italy, and Japan. Only permanent military occupation of these nations and permanent foreign control of their industries and trade could give stability to a peace made by using scissors and paste on the crazy map of Europe.

The peace signed in Paris in 1919 was not too unkind or vengeful. It was certainly far better than the cruel Brest-Litovsk Treaty which the Kaiser rammed down the throat of Soviet Russia in 1918. But if Versailles aimed to hold down Germany forever it was not unkind enough, and if it wished to heal Europe it was not kind enough. The alternatives that will face the world at the end of this war are the total annihilation of the defeated countries or a peace in a constructive spirit which will really prevent future wars.

It is going to be a hard job to give Europe a solid peace. The peace treaties that followed the first world war were built on three basic assumptions: unlimited national sovereignty, self-determination for the small nationalities which were pro-French, and the need of an anti-German coalition. Operating under these handicaps, Versailles was probably as good as it could have been. If the statesmen, starting with similar premises, assemble again to make another peace, they will face the same baffling situation which confronted Lloyd George, Clemenceau, Woodrow Wilson, and Orlando, and they may adopt similar measures. The events of 1939 proved that Czechoslovakia was defenseless without the Sudetenland, so the Sudetenland would have to go to Czechoslovakia; Germany would be left to nurse a grievance and Europe would have a festering sore. The races in Hungary and Rumania are settled in alternating belts: first Hungary proper, then an area inhabited by Rumanians, then an area inhabited by Hungarians, then Rumania proper. If you wish to give the area inhabited by Hungarians to Hungary you have to give her the intervening Rumanian belt, and then Rumania will protest. If you give the area inhabited by Rumanians to Rumania you must include the Hungarian belt in Rumania and that will be resented by Hungary. Resentment means border feuds, unrest, closed frontiers, hate-inspired alliances, and economic isolation. Such conditions plagued Europe between 1919 and 1939.

Europe is such a jumble of races, and the economic systems of its numerous countries are so interlaced and interdependent that it would seem to be the ideal place for a peace which lays far less emphasis on the things that divide and much more on the necessity of union. There are few perfect racial frontiers on the European continent, and every national frontier separates iron from coal, or factories from markets, or agricultural regions from their customers, or land-locked areas from the sea. In addition, every frontier is a tariff barrier.

Hitler has understood this. His New Order is the compulsory unification of Europe, and then of the whole world, under the heel of Nazi Germany. That is the plan. In actual life, Hitler succumbs to the temptation of ruthless map-carving. Thus, having conquered Yugoslovia, he gave a slice of that country to Bulgaria, a chunk to Italy, and took a big bite for Germany. That was in the spirit of Versailles against which Hitler had inveighed so fiercely; it was infintely worse than Versailles.

When the united anti-Axis nations win this war they will have to reject Hitler's method in Yugoslavia. Hitler compensated the victors and exterminated the vanquished. The Atlantic Charter promises something else. Implicit in the Charter is a peace which improves on Versailles because it deals not only with territorial changes and financial tribute but with social and economic questions. The peace of 1919 included errors of commission. Its chief fault, however, lay in its sins of omission; it failed to eliminate social injustice, economic friction, and international disunity.

THE SHAPE OF THE PEACE TO COME 235

The doctrines already promulgated by Churchill and Roosevelt and adopted by the anti-Axis coalition are a pledge that the next peace will be better than the last. Germany, Italy, and Japan have visited untold suffering upon mankind. Yet they may have to be given a better peace than they deserve simply because the peace they deserve might ruin the victorious peace-makers. We all live tightly together on a little island called the earth, and infections spread quickly from one country to another and from one continent to another. If we punish the defeated we punish ourselves.

What, then, is the shape of the peace to come?

Winston Churchill has never concealed his disinclination to formulate concrete peace terms while the war was still being waged. On his own, Churchill would not have promulgated the Atlantic Charter. The initiative which resulted in that document was President Roosevelt's. This much is freely admitted in London by persons in authority who add, however, that more than half the text of the Charter originated with Englishmen. When Churchill returned from his historic rendezvous with Roosevelt in a "spacious, land-locked bay," he reported on the event in a long broadcast to the British people. He first dealt with the eighth and last point of the Charter about disarmament of the enemy. He dramatically called the roll of the heroic conquered nations whose independence will be restored when hostilities cease, and he made a bow to Point Four concerning equal access to raw materials. But Point Five, child of Ernest Bevin's brain—"They desire . . . improved labor standards, economic advancement and social security"—was not mentioned, nor did Churchill even allude to "freedom from fear and want" or similar social phrases in the Charter.

The British contend that any attempt in wartime to enunciate definite war aims or peace terms would destroy their country's present unity and set Conservatives against progressives in fruitless debates about the future. There is some cogency in this argument. But my stay in England convinced me that the deeper reason for the Conservatives' reluctance to map the future is their attachment to the past. They fear that idealistic plans for the future might carry implications for the present.

For instance, if the British government announced that after the war there would be a European federation in which each state would have certain rights and representation, somebody might ask: Why don't you immediately offer that to India? The problem of the continent of India is not altogether unlike that of the European continent. Similarly, any outline of a perfect post-war social and economic system might reveal the imperfections of the present. It would reinforce the pressure which exists but is not strong enough to compel changes in the fundamental alignment of political power in England today.

It is true that no exact blueprint of the future peace is possible because nobody knows when the war will end and what the world will be like when the war does end. If peace aims had been published in 1939 during the German-Russian invasion of Poland they would have been very different from terms adopted in the light of the Nazi-Soviet war. How strong will Germany, Russia, and England be after the Nazi defeat? That will determine how much control is needed on the continent and who will exercise it. If Russia were very strong, the democratic allies might decide not to make Germany too weak. What share will America accept in the peace? That will shape the heart of the peace. Moreover, if the democratic belligerents started demarcating detailed boundaries and relationships in the post-war world, the well-known backstairs intrigues and lobbying of Paris in 1919 would begin. Greeks would pull wires against Bulgaria; Poles would demand East Prussia and feel cheated if they did not get it; Jews and Arabs would press rival claims for Palestine; Frenchmen would dispute Italy's right to this and that; and chaos would descend upon the chancelleries. It is never too late for such business.

The peace aims of the democracies cannot actually delineate frontiers. But it is not too soon to make sure that the men and women in the administrative offices and legislative bodies of the democracies are moved by the kind of sentiments, spirit, and principles which will produce a peace that can prevent a third world war. The young men who have to do the dying, the women who lose their men in wars, the mothers, the fathers, everybody must know that mankind is in grave danger. The world cannot afford to bleed itself white once every generation in a major war. Growing mechanization and modern invention make wars bloodier and bloodier. Twice in twenty-four years our civilization has launched massacres of the best young lives. There must be something wrong with the way we are organized, with the way we do things, with the people who do things for us. Society has had centuries in which to eliminate the causes of war but has failed to do so. While there is time we must look around and see where the fault lies. After 1918, nations quickly slipped back to where they were before 1914. Nothing fundamental was changed. The same rivalry between countries, the same powerful political and economic cliques within countries. No attempt was made to eradicate the causes of war. Consequently, we have this war. It could happen again. We could have a third world war.

The backward-looking appeasers and reactionaries said: We will fight the war when it comes to us. They would not fight it in China or Spain or Czechoslovakia. So it came to them. Now they say: We will make the peace when the time comes. They say that because they are reactionaries. They are afraid that clear thinking about the peace will expose their errors in the past. They are afraid the public will understand that the biggest threat to peace is to put privilege, property, and profit above human life, freedom, and justice. This is the lesson of world history between 1919 and 1939. It is not enough that the standpat defenders of the status quo helped get us into this war. They would lose us the war after it will have been won by the blood of millions of human beings. They did that once. They lost the first world war through the peace. Shall they be allowed to do it again? Shall the devotees of the past always kill our future?

War inspires men and women to the noblest deeds.

THE SHAPE OF THE PEACE TO COME 239

People are ready to die for an idea. Nations co-operate and forget what divides them. If only the idealism of wartime carried over into the peace we might have a real peace and a cleaner, better, happier world.

Two things can be done immediately: the public can voice its determination to have peace which goes deep, which goes beyond map-carving, which tackles the social, economic, and political causes of wars. The public can put into office and into positions of responsibility men and women to whom principles are dearer than privilege, and decency dearer than dollars, to whom the welfare of the common people is more important than the advancement of special interests, whose first allegiance is to human rights and not to property rights, who have a social consciousness and not merely a strong party-machine backing, who have ideals and love of humanity, who are not stick-in-the-mud old fogies with sclerotic brains and a devotion to everything that was, who are forward-looking and imaginative. There are such. The diplomatic services of the democracies should immediately be cleansed of the numerous snobs and appeasers whose pro-fascist attitude towards Abyssinia, Spain, and Czechoslovakia helped make this war. All servants of democracy should be persons who automatically translate democracy into the elimination of slums, equal opportunities for Negroes, social security, a minimum wage, no speculation in land values, development of economically backward areas, honest business practices, collective bargaining between employer and labor, free speech, free medical aid to the underprivileged, free higher education for the poor, freedom from racial discrimination, and freedom from worry over unemployment and old age. True democracy within countries would conduce to peace between countries.

No matter what promises and pronouncements are given now, the shape of the peace will depend on the persons who make it and on the mandate they get from the peoples who win in the bloody struggle. Fortunately, the peace this time will take form slowly, step by step, and at each step an educated vocal public opinion could show its approval or disapproval and thus influence the future course of their government's action. A large number of political thinkers in Britain is inclined to oppose holding a peace conference right after hostilities cease. There may not be a peace treaty when this war ends. The peace should grow gradually out of life instead of shooting up into completed form in the hothouse atmosphere of a peace conference.

The first move when fighting stops will have to be the feeding of Europe and Asia. This time the democratic allies will not repeat the mistake of continuing the blockade after the war. Many people in many countries will be starving and the prey of epidemics by the time the war is finished. Most of the relief work will be the duty or responsibility of the United States which alone is likely to have the necessary surpluses. In London and Washington concrete plans for this humanitarian activity are already being drafted.

Simultaneously, the victorious countries will occupy Germany, Italy, and Japan, or only Germany and Italy if the war in Europe is won before Japan is conquered, and proceed to confiscate their arms. There is general

THE SHAPE OF THE PEACE TO COME 241

agreement that this is inevitable and a widespread feeling that it is desirable. Here the trouble will begin. The British may not hate the Germans. Apparently, however, German bombs are less hate-provoking than the physical presence of Germans, and the Poles, Dutch, Czechs, and other victims of Nazi occupation do hate Germans passionately. Their alleged ambition, the moment German power crumbles, is to slaughter the maximum number of available Germans.

Retribution is necessary; criminals should be punished. Hitler, his fellow-gangster Nazi leaders, his generals, and the officials in occupied territories who are today directing horrible massacres of hostages, deliberate starvation of subject peoples, planned extermination of whole districts, and the universal enslavement of defeated nations should pay for their crimes. It has been suggested that a list be kept of these German, Italian, Spanish, Hungarian, Rumanian, and Japanese monsters and their Quislings, that the list be published as it grows, and that the persons whose names appear on it be regularly warned that when the war is over they will be overtaken by the fate they richly deserve. It will be a long list. Some would go beyond it and shoot millions of Germans after this war; I have heard suggestions that from three to thirty million Germans be shot. This would be the opening gun of their new peace. And, since the worst Nazis are the young Nazis and those who have been inculcated with Nazi doctrine in schools, the blood bath of peace, I presume, would begin with the wholesale killing of children. Such obscene notions, I hope, will be scotched before they are translated into even limited action. The troops which occupy the defeated fascist countries will keep order, prevent murder, and arrest the responsible criminals.

The reason for occupying the defeated nations is to permit a breathing spell for tempers to cool, bitterness to evaporate, economic rehabilitation to commence, and governments to be organized by progressive, anti-fascist forces in defeated countries. These governments will then proceed to do what the German Republic after 1919 did not do: destroy the power for future harm in the hands of the Junkers, militarists, industrialists, and old civil servants. The political agents accompanying the armies of occupation will have to be enlightened enough to see the relation between these internal social reforms and world amity. Meanwhile, the contours of the peace will gradually emerge.

But who is to send armies of occupation into the defeated countries? This will be the first knotty political problem. The leading candidates are Great Britain, Russia, if she is among the victors, and the United States.

I believe Winston Churchill, shrewd political genius, has sensed the potential affinity which may spring up between post-war Russia and England. British Conservatives, though eternally suspicious of Russia's socialistic origins, might nevertheless be capable of real friendship for a nationalistic Russia serving as a convenient counterpoise to the Germans of Central Europe. The rekindling of the ancient Teuton-Slav feud would compel Russia and Germany to face one another apprehensively and jealously for many years. That would give

THE SHAPE OF THE PEACE TO COME 243

England security against Germany. Thus preoccupied in Europe, Russia, moreover, could become the ally of Britain in the Middle East after the pattern of 1907-1917. The present Anglo-Russian condominium in Iran is a foretaste of such a possible development. If Moscow consented to enter an alliance of this nature, British statesmanship might accede to a Russian occupation of Eastern Europe with a view, ultimately, to the re-establishment of the Slav states of Poland, Czechoslovakia, Bulgaria, and Yugoslavia inside a kind of big-brother Muscovite protectorate euphemistically called a Slav regional federation.

The execution of this scheme depends on Russia's internal condition after the war. If she is exhausted by the fighting, her role in the peace will be smaller. Peace settlements are the handiwork not of those who contributed most to the victory but of those who have most strength left after the victory. It is more than likely, should Hitler and Stalin continue locked in a death grapple on through 1942 or even 1943, that Russia will lack the energy and resources to do anything beyond her own frontiers.

The main task of making the coming world peace will fall to England and the United States even if Russia does influence the situation in Eastern Europe. Since England's power will have been seriously depleted by the war, the British will lean heavily on America.

England alone cannot protect the peace. Most English people are pessimistic about their post-war economic outlook. An Englishwoman said to me, "I would not leave England during the war, but I would not want to stay in England after the war." There will be a great surge in England to emigrate to the Western Hemisphere when the peace comes. The British expect foreign trade difficulties and unemployment. They will need American aid after the war. The war is creating more understanding between England and the U. S. A. In the course of the war many parts of the British Empire are sure to be drawn very close to the United States. Intimate Anglo-American relations in the peace will be necessary, and if they are not maintained it will be a disaster to the world.

England has traditionally exercised her world influence through balance-of-power politics. Before this war, the British attempted to dominate the international situation through an Anglo-French coalition. The collapse and weakness of France preclude a resumption of that arrangement. Certain British statesmen, therefore, wish to substitute an Anglo-American balance of power for the defunct Anglo-French balance of power, and to supplement it with an Anglo-Russian balance of power in special areas.

If I were asked what was the first cause of this war and of the war of 1914-1918, I would reply, balance-of-power politics. History shows that every effort at balance induces an effort to unbalance the balance, and the result is war.

Immediately after the first world war, France was strong and Germany very weak. England accordingly began to throw her weight on the side of Germany in order to re-establish a European equilibrium. Subsequently, Germany became too powerful and intract-

THE SHAPE OF THE PEACE TO COME 245

able. Therefore, Britain transferred her weight to the French scale. That was the alignment on September 3, 1939. When the war ends, it will be impossible to balance Germany against France. The French Republic fell in 1940 because successive French government had refused to collect the taxes, introduce the social reforms and adopt a foreign policy which would have enabled the country to resist German and Italian fascism. France could have been stronger economically than she was when Germany attacked her. Nevertheless, Germany is by her size, natural resources, and geographic position a more powerful country than France. After the war, England will of course be interested in resurrecting a democratic France to partially offset Germany. But France plus Britain are no longer an adequate balance against Germany. So an alternative is canvassed: balance Germany against Russia, and balance the whole world against an Anglo-American partnership. This may sound all right. But it is a perpetuation of the old system which sets nation against nation and group of nations against group of nations; it puts a premium on competing alliances, and on armaments with which to defend existing supremacy. In this rivalry is the seed of future wars. The Anglo-French entente after 1919 sounded just as good and seemed just as mighty as an Anglo-American fusion will after this war. It too was surrounded with idealistic words about devotion to democracy and about rivers of blood spilled on the battlefield in a common cause. But then came the aeroplane as a decisive weapon of war; the economic rise of several countries altered the balance of international political power; appeasement, child of class interest and pacifism, blinded governments to impending assaults on the balance. That added up to the second world war. Every balance of power is precarious, temporary, and conducive to uncertainty.

This does not mean that England and America should not collaborate closely. They must collaborate, but not as England and France did after 1919. England and France collaborated in the League of Nations. But the League was never an organism, it was only an organization. Diplomats and politicians met at intervals at Geneva, made speeches, exchanged memoranda, and if it suited England or France or both, the League adopted certain resolutions or even, rarely, took certain actions. It was like a Rotary Club whose members function as a unit for a lunch or an evening and then disperse and go their separate ways leaving committees, perhaps, to do charity or educational work. Similarly, the League had its information department, its valuable International Labor Office, its health service, and so forth. In the important business, however, of saving the world from war, the League was just not there. It merely offered a place and platform for old-style balance-of-power intrigues and wire-pulling. The countries were not knitted together; they occasionally came together. The League was not an international federation; it was nationalism behaving politely because the public was looking.

It has been said that if the United States had joined the League of Nations, things would have been different. Undoubtedly. But the British and French themselves could have created a saner world had they been sane. The surrender to Japan in China in 1932 was not America's fault. England and France—not America—were chiefly to blame for Abyssinia, Spain, and Czechoslovakia. The paramount consideration is not whether two nations combine or three nations combine. The real question is what prompts them to combine, against whom they combine, and who combines against them. Did England and France ever want America to join with them in redistributing raw materials, and did America refuse? No. They never proposed it. Did Chamberlain and Daladier say to the White House: Let us take counsel together and stop the fascist aggressors? No. They did exactly the opposite. They reinforced the appeasers in Washington and in American embassies abroad. They could have done the same thing if America had been a member of the League of Nations.

In the future too, America's role in the peace will depend on the purpose of international politics and on the nature of the peace. If two or three nations unite to perpetuate their supremacy and create the impression of trying to dominate, then two or three other nations will unite to form a balance against them. The two groups will seesaw up and down until some day one will fall off the board and there will be a war. Only world unity can extirpate this evil.

How will world unity grow out of the blood and ruin of this war?

It cannot come overnight. Some persons sketch the

ideal peace. I think it is more desirable to deal with realistic possibilities or probabilities.

We might as well make up our minds that if America does not participate in an enlightened peace which improves the world there will be no peace. There will be another major war and we will be drawn into it as we were twice in twenty-four years. The United States may be in a mood of self-centered isolation and disgust with Europe when the hostilities cease. If that induces America to remain aloof from post-war reconstruction we will have wasted half our war effort. Moreover, the economy of the United States would suffer.

Peace will find Europe and Asia flat on their backs. This is a very destructive war. When the guns are silenced, foreign nations will lack the raw materials, capital, machinery, the faith, and perhaps even the engineering skill and manpower to reconstruct their territories. America will have to make a major contribution towards rebuilding them. Who will pay America? For a long time—nobody. But it will cost America less to rebuild Europe for nothing than to finance our worst business depression if we did not rebuild Europe and instead closed our factories and sent home our workingmen. This war need not be followed by the slump which usually follows a war. On the contrary, the war could be succeeded by an era of great prosperity in America. We could quickly reconvert our industry to civilian purposes, and after satisfying real domestic needs, export the large quantities of goods which the devastated countries will require for their restoration.

THE SHAPE OF THE PEACE TO COME 249

It will be a sort of world W.P.A. That will prevent a depression. That will also bring social changes in America.

In the long run, and, also, in the not very long run, the reconstruction of Europe will react to America's real benefit. Just as the world cannot be half slave and half free so it cannot comfortably be half poor and half prosperous. An impoverished Europe and Asia would reduce the world's standard of living. That includes America's standard of living.

An underdeveloped Poland and a backward, starving China retard humanity's progress. In peace, Britain, though highly industrialized and very rich, was America's best customer. America will not lose, she will only gain if other countries get rich with her help. That is excellent business. To raise China, India, and Russia to America's level of well-being would keep the world's factories busy for a century. That would be the solidest foundation of future peace. It will be good for America to lease-lend Europe and Asia back to a normal economic existence. This time we must be in the peace right away and in the right way.

With American armies of occupation in Europe, with America sending large quantities of food and industrial commodities to Europe, and with America devoting itself to a solution of Europe's old problems, American economists, business men, and statesmen will meet in frequent consultations with European, including British, representatives. The views of the Americans will carry considerable weight. They will point out, in one instance, that a certain tariff barrier interferes with reconstruction and trade and ought to be wiped out. They will suggest that A and B, two neighboring countries, one rich in raw materials and factories, the other a big farming nation, ought to dovetail their economic systems, and if they did they could count on more American support. Purely by a concrete engineering approach to the problems of reconstruction, the United States could exercise a very salutary influence on the reshaping of Europe's new life.

Inevitably, the Europeans must say to America, What about your own tariff? "Our high tariff," said Sumner Welles, Under-Secretary of State of the United States, on October 8, 1941, "reached out to virtually every corner of the earth and brought poverty and despair to innumerable communities. . . . The resultant misery, bewilderment and resentment, together with equally pernicious contributing causes, paved the way for the rise of the very dictatorships which have plunged the entire world into war." No informed person will dispute this statement. The American high tariff and America's business depression which began in 1929 had more to do with the coming of Hitler than the Versailles Treaty or any innate perversion of German character. America is so powerful and wealthy that what happens in Washington, New York, and Chicago reverberates in every distant land.

Is the United States prepared to drastically lower or entirely cancel its tariff? If not, our participation in world peace will be abortive. This is no longer only a question of domestic politics. The fate of the earth

THE SHAPE OF THE PEACE TO COME 251

and the to be or not to be of the third world war depend on it.

An Anglo-American customs union has been suggested. A vast free-trade area, embracing the American economic empire, if Latin America be included, and the British Empire, seems like a magnificent, inspiring conception. Would it permit American exports to enter Australia duty free while German and Russian exports paid a tariff in Australia? Germany and Russia might not like that. Would American textiles be admitted where Japanese textiles were barred? The countries excluded from the Anglo-American customs union might be threatened with economic ruin. That might lead to a competing customs union consisting of Russia, Germany, Japan, and so forth. Any union which is incomplete means disunity and rivalry.

A customs union of America with Britain could easily be made so attractive that everybody else would willingly join on the very first day. Those that stayed out would soon see the benefits and knock at the door. But if all countries tore down their tariff walls, efficient, industrialized countries like the United States and Germany would swamp the partly-industrialized nations with goods and ruin their industries. Places like Yugoslavia, Turkey, and Chile, which want to industrialize because industrialized nations are more prosperous, would not be able to maintain their own factories in the face of foreign competition. Agricultural countries with cheap labor would undersell domestic farmers in other countries. The consequent chaos and catastrophes would be very great. To avoid these difficulties, a world entirely free of tariff barriers would have to get together and plan its economic life. A universal customs union would make planning indispensable. Planning would be the dawn of real sanity and world peace.

Anthony Eden, British Foreign Secretary, who often talks about the peace in social terms, said on May 29, 1941, "Let no one suppose that we, for our part, intend to return to the chaos of the old world." In the new post-war world, "social security will be our policy abroad not less than at home," he added. "We shall seek to achieve this in ways which will interfere as little as possible with the proper liberty of each country over its own economic fortunes." The war and the new perspective which the war has given us of the pre-war period have aroused a widespread feeling of the mutuality of responsibility. Every man is every other man's keeper. That is true of any village, city and nation. It is equally true of the whole world. "We have learned a lesson in the interregnum between wars," Mr. Eden declared. "We know that no escape can be found from the curse which has been lying on Europe except by creating and preserving economic health in every country." Emphasis on "every." This war marks the beginning of the breakdown of national egoism. All countries stand and fall together.

World customs union. World economic planning. International economic health. These are the first step to a stable peace. The people are ready. Now the leaders must act.

Planning in a free-trade world cannot mean a limita-

THE SHAPE OF THE PEACE TO COME 253

tion of production or employment. That would defeat its purpose. There is room everywhere for more production. I asked a girl in an American college recently how many dresses she had. "Six," she replied. A Russian girl is happy to have one. If every Chinaman wore pants the world would be forced to grow more cotton. Hundreds of millions of men, women, and children on this civilized planet of ours are inadequately fed, clothed, housed, and educated. We have the labor and the raw materials. We have not had the proper kind of organization, distribution, and planning.

Under a world plan, markets would not be open to anybody who could reach them with his goods. Raw materials and markets would be apportioned by an international board of scientific managers, not so as to destroy industries or farm production but so as to stimulate both, to create new markets, and to develop retarded areas. A country that refused to submit its raw materials to the general allocation would not be interfered with. It would only be barred from outside markets. No nation is stronger economically than all the others combined. No nation is economically independent. Every country has to buy and sell abroad. These imports and exports would be put in a pool and distributed according to natural wealth, plant facilities and trained labor supplies.

The existence of a world planning board would have enormous political importance. Its control over the distribution of raw materials and markets would be a potential sanction against aggressors. If a country were stocking up for war, the records of the board would show it and the effort could be stopped.

Thus, world economic planning would be the first exciting experiment in practical internationalism. It would involve a slight abridgement of national sovereignty. If the nations accept this abridgement and if planning operates to the obvious benefit of all, as it must, the world would be prepared for the next step in international co-operation. World unity can only be achieved gradually. It might be fine if all nations, by one decision, surrendered all their sovereignty and merged into one world government with one world senate and one world president. I believe it more than likely, however, that they will not surrender all their sovereignty until they have all surrendered a little and see that it works. An Anglo-American union now would probably be regarded by many Germans as a form of imperialism designed to dominate them. They and others would look with far less suspicion on a union if they were all present at its birth instead of being asked to join what had already been organized by the two most powerful victorious nations. Internationalism should be taught in easy stages beginning, immediately after the war, with inescapable economic collaboration.

Meanwhile, the armies occupying the countries defeated in the war could be reduced in size as normal life returned. Ultimately, they would be withdrawn entirely and become the nucleus of an international peace-time police force equipped with all the weapons of war. Germany, Japan, and Italy would be disarmed. The victors would have an international police force

THE SHAPE OF THE PEACE TO COME

which they could trust because it was theirs. Therefore, they too might disarm themselves and depend for protection on the international force. One or more countries might refuse to contribute to this force and might insist on having their own armaments. The problem then would be to maintain the international force at a strength great enough to enable it to effectively defend any territory which a non-participating member might attack.

The international force would raise problems of sovereignty. The force would have to be stationed in many countries. But since it would not be subject to any one government it would not be subject to the government of the territory where it was stationed. On the other hand, the presence of the force would be a guarantee against aggression, and at least the little countries would welcome it for that very reason. Perhaps therein is the kernel of a solution: the international police force would be quartered in weaker countries which have in the past known what it means to be invaded and which would be glad to have the protection of an impartial, super-national fighting machine.

When internationalism in practice brings safety and prosperity, people will ask for more of it. Eventually, sincere co-operation between nations will become the rule in peacetime rather than the exception. Europe has learned a great deal since this war started, and it will have learned much more before the war is over. As Hitler's tanks and planes rushed across frontiers, nations realized how inadequate those frontiers were. The frontiers embarrassed them in peacetime but did not help in war.

Nationalism is a strong force and sometimes it is a healthy force. But narrow self-centered nationalism has ended so often in the death of nations that people are apparently ready to modify it. The brand of nationalism which prompted Colonel Beck, Poland's foreign minister, to aid Hitler in the partition of Czechoslovakia has proved to be a boomerang; the partition of Czechoslovakia in 1938 led straight to the partition of Poland in 1939. No one can deny this. Everybody saw it happen. Millions of Poles and Czechs are today paying for it. As a result, the Czech and Polish exile governments in London have scrapped their traditional animosity and are creating an intimate relationship of collaboration. In like manner, the Greeks and Yugoslavs, in the persons of their refugee officials, have agreed to form a customs union when they return to their native lands.

Europe has paid a high price for disunity. Hence the readiness to strike out into new paths.

It is not wise, however, to be too optimistic. The factors tending towards disruption are numerous. The pull back towards the old will remain when the war ends. Racial pride and national hate die hard as long as they can be used to whip up passions which aid governments in their tasks.

Mussolini, for instance, refused to parcel out the large estates and satisfy the land-hungry Italian peasantry. This made the peasants easy victims of his imperialistic propaganda for a place in the African sun where he

THE SHAPE OF THE PEACE TO COME

promised them farms and employment. Wars may be rooted in national feelings and traditions. But sometimes they spring from unresolved social and economic problems within countries. Germany's manufacturers wanted raw materials and markets. Germany's military caste wanted work and power. Germany's big farmers and estate-owning Junkers did not want foreign farm land. But they were strong enough politically to thwart Chancellor Bruening's and Hitler's early intentions of breaking up the estates. Consequently, the little German farmer felt cheated and cramped; he yearned to go places, to do things. "Colonies," whispered the imperialists. "The Ukraine," whispered the Nazis. The German urban middle class was suffering from the rise of monopolies and mammoth trusts. It was hit hard by the post-1929 depression. It feared Communism. Hitler rolled all these German desires, fears and discontents into a giant meat ball and peppered it generously with Nazi doctrine.

Revolutions and wars are born in national soil. Foreign politics reflect domestic politics. Peace is built on sensible, smooth relations between countries. But unless each country is well adjusted within itself it cannot adjust to other countries. The key to future peace is happier social, economic and political conditions inside all nations.

The conservatives have had decades in which to deal with these difficulties. But they were apparently too handicapped by their own interests to take a broader view. If property interests and money interests continue after this war to pursue the old chase for power, raw materials and markets there are bound to be frictions, wounds and wars.

Real democracies would find a way of preventing wars. Real democracies would be immune to the pressure of special interests and special lobbies. This war was made by open-eyed brown, black and red dictatorships and by blind colorless conservatives. There is just one peaceway that has not been tried: democracy. The United States, Great Britain, France and other countries have had a considerable measure of democracy. But French Foreign Minister Bonnet was much closer to the Two Hundred Families than to the millions of peasants and workers. Neville Chamberlain was first of all a Birmingham business man. French big business and the French banks were able to kill the reforms of the Popular Front which was a mild New Deal and, too, to retard rearmament. Even such incomplete democracy is better far than any dictatorship. But that kind of democracy is not good enough and not effective enough in stopping wars. In the last analysis, an international free trade customs union, international economic planning and world organization for peace depend on how much direct influence the people exercise over governments and how much direct and indirect influence the conservative business interests exercise over governments. Many forces will resist customs unions and planning and the domestic changes they will make necessary. We must see to it that before the war is over every person who may have a hand in shaping the peace and thus shaping our future life will be a convinced, enthusiastic democrat free from any mental reservations about real democracy and free from any ties except those that bind him to the welfare of the nation as a whole. We must see to that now. In time of war prepare for peace.

The end of this war will offer mankind its great opportunity. The war will exhaust the world, and it is not too optimistic to expect that for ten years after this conflict there will not be another major war simply because most countries will not have the energy to start one. That is the decade in which to build a new world for peace. It is a task for youth and the youthful, for the mothers and fathers whose sons and daughters will die in the third world war if this opportunity is missed. It is a task for all.

After the black horrors of this war, every sensitive human being will see the necessity of establishing a firm, solid, and good peace. Such a peace is possible. It will cost less than the third world war.

INDEX

INDEX

Acland, Sir Richard, 121, 122, 126, 133-35
aggression, 177-79, 226-28
air raids on England, 28-33
airplanes, aerodromes, English, 58
 American, Roosevelt production schedule, 217
 ammunition, English, 53
 at Lisbon, 15
 aviators, English and German, 213-14
 bombers for victory, 212-17
 Clipper, passage by, and landing, 4-10
 clothing, English airmen's, 51-52
 flight in a "Maggie," 60-65
 guns, English airmen's, 50
 Hurricanes, 50, 53
 Royal Air Force, 46-65, 119
 Spitfires, 53
Alexander, A. V., 85, 94
Allen, Jay, 15
America. See United States
American Magazine, 141
Amery, Leopold, 94, 189
 linguist, 99-100
Anderson, Sir John, 30-31, 96, 98-99
 shelter, 30-31
anti-Fascist nations, 209
 defeat of Germany by attack, 219
 resources, 209-10
appeasers, 158-59, 176-77, 238, 247
Atlantic Charter, the (Eight Points), 104, 229-31, 234-35
Attlee, Clement Richard, 86, 93-94, 95
aviators. *See* Airplanes
Axis, adherence of Hungary, Slovakia, and Rumania, 146

Axis (Cont.)
 defeat dependent on attack, 219
 resources, 209-10
Azores, 7-10

balance-of-power politics, 244-45, 247
Baldwin, Stanley, 113, 117, 125, 126
Balkans, 145, 147
Baltic states, 158
Bank of England, 113
Beaverbrook, Lord, 38, 85-88, 96
Belgium, 148
Bermuda, 6-7
Bevan, Aneurin, 96, 131
Bevan, Mr. and Mrs. Aneurin, 30
Bevin, Ernest, 85, 86, 87, 88, 90, 96, 235
Biggers, John D., 132
Bingham, Lieutenant Colonel R. C., 118
Black Record, by Lord Vansittart, 224
black-outs, 53-54
Bolshevism. *See* Union of Soviet Socialist Republics
bombers. *See* airplanes
bombing of England, 28-33
Bonnet, Georges, 258
Boudberg, Countess Moura, 74
Bracken, Brendan, 107, 129
Brauchitsch, General Walther von, 199
Brest-Litovsk Treaty, 232
Britain. *See* England
British Agent, by Bruce Lockhart, 74
British Broadcasting Corporation, 69-77
Bruening, Chancellor, 257
Bulgaria, 146, 147, 166

INDEX

cabinet, Churchill's, 84-108
Campbell, Sir Gerald, 37
Carol, King of Rumania, 219
casino at Estoril, Portugal, 11-12
Chamberlain, Neville, 25, 36, 73, 83, 89, 97, 100, 106, 107, 117, 125, 126, 127, 225, 245, 258
    era, 22
Chicago *Daily News*, 14
Churchill, Winston, 38, 71, 77, 81-108, 112, 117, 120, 189, 190, 207, 224, 235, 236
    and Hess, 26
    and war, 83
    as a broadcaster, 35
    as a speaker, 82-83
    Atlantic Charter, 229-31
    cabinet, 84-108
    defender of liberty, 93
    denunciation of, on German radio, 45
    distrust of, former, 125
    genius, political, 82
    lack of adventure, 104-05
    man of words and action, 82-83
    obliviousness to impending social changes, 107
    opposition to discussion of terms of peace, 226, 235-36
    successor, possible, 96
    trust of the people, 22-23
    weakness as a producer and administrator, 81-82, 84
Citrine, Sir Walter, 89
Clemenceau, Georges, 233
Clipper, passage by, and landing, 4-10
coal mining, English, 43-44, 123-24, 130
Cockerell, Sir Sydney, 71-72
Combes, B. L., 113-14
Comintern (Third International), 164-65
common man, cult of the, English, 33-38
Communism, 160-66, 167
conservatives and war, 257-58
co-operation, international, 252-53
countries, occupied, 205-06
Cranborne, Viscount, 106-07
Crete, 147

crimes, war, retribution for, 241-43
Cripps, Sir Stafford, 96-97
cult, English, of the common man, 33-38
Cunard, Nancy, 74
customs union, proposed, 251-52
Cvetkovitch, Premier, 147
Czechoslovakia, 256

Daily Herald, London, 89
Daily News, Chicago, 14
Daily Worker, London, 92
Daladier, Edouard, 247
Dalton, Dr. Hugh, 94, 202
Darlan, Admiral, 206
Davies, Joseph E., 152
democracies, defeat of Axis dependent on attack, 219
    Fascist view, 178-79
democracy, and war, 258
    doubts concerning, 219-20
    essentials of, 239
    real, 258-59
Derzhavin, Professor, 165
dictatorships, 160-61, 226-28
    defeat not enough to cure the world, 229
    products of world changes, 228-29
Dieckhoff, Hans, 11, 12
Dimitrov, Georgi, 165
disarmament, German, 230-31
Dobbie, William, 39, 44
domination and leadership, difference between, 186
Dos Passos, John, 76
Dunkirk, retreat from, 34-35, 190-91

Economist, The, 95, 108, 109, 113, 116
Eden, Anthony, 26, 38, 96, 97-98, 100, 114, 252
    on future peace, 230
    on social security, 38
Egypt, 147
Eight Points, The. *See* Atlantic Charter
England, aims, war, 36-45
    air force and army, 54-55

INDEX

England (Cont.)
    allowances, proposed, to large families, 100
    and Hitler, 24
    and the United States, 101, 135-36; collaboration, post-war, 246
    army; and air force, 54-55; "old school tie," and modernization of army, 118-20
    balance-of-power politics, 244-45
    bombing of, 28-33
    business, and economic system, 121-36
    cabinet, Churchill's, 84-108
    class prejudices and barriers, 116-21
    coal mining, and handling, 43-44, 123-24
    coalowners, holding back of better product, 130
    conscription of resources, for victory, 210-12
    Conservatives, obliviousness of social changes, 107-08
    cult of the common man, 33-38
    defensive in Europe, 191-93
    democracy, aims of, 37; future of, 111-35
    diplomatic service, 114
    economic system, and business, 121-36
    education, 117
    employer-worker production councils, 128-29
    Excess Profits Tax, 129-30, 131
    factories, antiquated and modern, 124
    faith in victory, 189-90
    Fascists, 92
    food, war-time, 105-06
    future, 111-35
    Home Guard, 42-44; jokes on, 76-77
    Home Secretary, functions of, 90-92
    in war time, 16-18, 21-136
    industry, conscription of, 131-32
    invasion not part of Hitler's 1941 plan, 143-45

England (Cont.)
    labor, loyalty of, 127-28
    lack of arms for offense, 191-92
    leaders, present and future, 111-12
    leadership, monopoly of, 111-13, 125-26; weak, 112-13
    liberties in war time, 92-93
    man power, lack of, 132
    manufacturers' motives, 130-31
    morals in war time, 32-33
    northern, plants and factories in, 41
    on peace with Hitler, 27-29
    opposition to statement of peace terms, 226, 235-36
    "P's," five, 130-31
    Parliament, 38; seats for sale, 114-17
    politics, 114-17
    post-war, 243-44; and Soviet Russia, 242
    premier, possible, after Churchill, 96
    production, speed-up, 132
    production minister, need for, 86-87
    property, conscription of, 131-32
    religion in war time, 32-33
    Royal Air Force, 49-65, 119
    schools, 117
    Select Committee on National Expenditure, 127, 128, 135
    songs, war, 55
    treatment of enemy airman, 46
    two million versus forty-eight million, 111, 118
    unprepared for war, 126-27
    work at cross-purposes, 133-35
Estoril, Portugal, casino, 11-12
Europe, federation, proposed, 236
    intermingling of races and nations, 233-34
    invasion by anti-Fascists, plan for, 217-18
    reconstruction, post-war, 248-50

Fascism, 226-28
Fascist nations, 193-209
    aggression, 177-79

INDEX

Fascist nations (Cont.)
  goal, world domination, 178
"Fifth Columns," anti-Axis, 219
Financial News, 128, 129, 130
Finland, 139-40, 158
Fischer, Louis, *Men and Politics*, 153
Fisher, Sir Warren, 33-34
France, capitulation, 139, 206-07
  conservatives and the Popular Front, 258
  fall, causes of, 245
  letters from, in sympathy with England, 206-07
  losses in the war, 191
  Popular Front, 258
  Unoccupied, 8
Franco, Francisco, 227, 228
  See also Spain
Fulmars, the, 8-9
Fyfe, Major Maxwell, 116

Gamarnick, General, 153
Gandhi, Mohandas Karamchand, 103
geographical adjustments after the war, 231-32
Germany, aid from occupied countries, 208
  aim in the war, 25
  aims, according to Goebbels, 175-76
  air force exaggerated, 215
  anti-Hitler Germans, 13, 204-05, 228
  army, dual-purpose, 133; impaired, 217-18; not caste-ridden, 119
  assets and liabilities in occupied countries, 205-06
  attack on Soviet Russia, 27-28, 139-60
  blockade, 202
  bombing, plan for, 215-17
  clothing situation, 201
  conditions, domestic, 195-205
  defeat in 1918, 202-04
  defeatism, 204
  disarmament, 230-31
  food situation, 200

Germany (Cont.)
  German race blamed for wars, by some Englishmen, 224-26
  Germans, post-war hatred of, 241
  guilt, sole, for first world war, question of, 225-26
  hatred for, absent in England, 224
  "Hitlerite" or "Nazi," 163
  impulses toward war, 257
  leaders, 112
  Nazi war crimes, retribution for, 241-43
  Nazis, 13; "master race," 12
  occupation, post-war, 240-41
  partition, proposed, 232
  prisoners, German, in England, treatment of, 46
  rebuilding, 121-22
  scientists, exiled, working against Hitler, 214
Goebbels, Paul Joseph, 25
  appeal for clothing for the army, 201
  confession of aims, 175-76
  on 1918 defeat, 203
  on the war, 196-99
Great Britain. *See* England
Greece, 147, 219, 256
Greenwood, Arthur, 25, 86, 94, 95
Gunston, Sir Derrick, 115

Halifax, Lord, 38, 72, 96
Harsch, Joseph C., *Pattern of Conquest*, 119
"have" and "have-not" nations, 177
Henderson, Nevile, 83
Herbert, Sam, 31
Hess, Rudolph, flight to Scotland, 26-27
Hindenburg, General, 203
Hitler, Adolf, aim, 25
  and war, 83
  blow to German faith in, 199-200
  calculations, war, 142-46
  challenge to capitalism and democracy, 37-38

INDEX

Hitler, Adolf (Cont.)
  crimes, war, retribution for, 241-43
  distrust of people, 23
  error, military, crowning, 191
  hatred for, in England, 224
  hold on his people, 204
  man of words and action, 82
  New Order, 36, 178, 229, 234
  no living with, 24
  plan to invade Russia, 145
  promise to break up estates, 257
  rise to power, 179
  self-justification, 227-28
  "wave of the future," 175
Hoare, Sir Samuel, 96, 108
Hopkins, Harry, 141
Hore-Belisha, Leslie, 232
  reforms, and dismissal, 119-20
Horta, 5-6, 7-10
Hungary, 146, 147
Hurricanes (planes), 50-53

India, 94, 101-03, 236
  industrialization, 125
International Labor Office, 246
international meeting place, last, 11-12
internationalism, practical, 211-12, 254-56
Iran (Persia), 98, 243
Iraq, 147, 149
isolationists, 176-77
Italy, entry into the war, 183
  fate dependent on Germany's, 218
  occupation, post-war, 240-41
  peasants, Mussolini's promises to, 256-57
  weakness and losses, 194-95
Ivan the Terrible, 162
Izvestia, Moscow, 150, 161

Jameson, Margaret Storm, 21, 73, 74
  on the Germans, 225
Japan, 13, 142, 159, 160
  attack on the United States, 173-75, 182-85
  defeat more difficult than Germany's, 218

Japan (Cont.)
  economic condition, 208-09
  occupation, post-war, 240-43

Kennedy, Joseph P., 73
Kerr, Walter, 76
Kirkpatrick, Ivone, 26-27
Koestler, Arthur, 74, 93

Laski, Harold J., 38
Latin America, 181
leadership and domination, difference between, 186
League of Nations, 246-47
Leigh, Vivien, 105
Lenin, Nikolai, 164
  and national culture, 163
  internationalism, 161
Lindbergh, Charles A., 215
Lisbon, 10-15
Litvinov, Maxim, 155, 157
Lloyd George, David, 36, 41, 84, 189, 230, 233
  on big and little men, 87
  on Churchill, 103-04
Lloyd George, Major Gwilym, 106
Lockhart, Bruce, *British Agent*, 74
London, bombing of, 30-34
London *Daily Herald*, 89
London *Daily Worker*, 92
London speaking, 69-77
London *Sunday Times*, 224
Londonderry, Lord, 107
Lozovsky, S., 148
Ludendorff, General, 203

MacCarthy, Desmond, 74
Macaulay, Rose, 74-76
Maisky, Ivan, 74, 99
Mann, Erika, 74
Mannerheim, Marshal, 158
Margesson, David, 84, 95, 118
markets, world, development of, 253
Martin, Kingsley, 74
Marx, Karl, 161
Mass Organization, 96
materials, raw, 230, 253
  and war, 178
Men and Politics, by Louis Fischer, 153

INDEX

Metaxas, Premier, 219
Meynell, Viola, 71-72
militarism, 226-28
Molotov, Vyacheslav, 145, 146, 148
Morgan, Louise, 74
Moore-Brabazon, Colonel, 85
Morrison, Herbert, 89, 90-93
   defender of Liberty, 93
Moscow *Izvestia*, 150, 161
Moscow *Red Star*, 148
Mosley, Sir Oswald, 92
Munich agreement, 126-27
Mussolini, Benito, distrust of people, 23
   opposition to, 194
   promises to Italian peasantry, 256
   taking over of Italy, 178-79

Nation, The, New York, 105
nationalism, peril in, 256
   stubborn, 256
Nazis. *See* Germany
Nazi air pilot, incident of, 70-71
Nazis in Portugal, 11-12
Nehru, Jawaharlal, 103, 104
New Order, 36, 178, 229, 234
New Statesman and Nation, 101, 113
New York Times, 149, 175, 196
Norman, Sir Montagu, 107
Norway, 148, 192

occupied countries, 205-06
Oliver, Vic, 77
Order, New, 36, 178, 229, 234
Orlando, Vittorio, 233
Otto, Archduke, 220
Out of the People, by J. B. Priestley, 36

P. E. N., 71-74
P's, five, 130-31
Palestine, 147, 237
Paton, Reverend William W., 31-33
Pattern of Conquest, by Joseph C. Harsch, 119
Paul, Prince of Yugoslavia, 147
peace and peace terms, essentials of, 239

peace and peace terms (Cont.)
   foundations of, 257
   geographical adjustments not a guarantee, 231-32
   ideal or practical, 248
   punishment excluded, 231-32
   reparations excluded, 231
   shape of, 223-59
   temporary, negotiated, 176
   treaties after the first world war, 233
Peel, Honorable George, 72
Persia (Iran), 98, 243
Pétain, Marshal Henri Philippe, 206, 207
Peter, King of Yugoslavia, 147
Peter the Great, 161, 165
Picture Post, 113-14
planes. *See* Airplanes
planning for world co-operation, 252-54
Poland, 166, 256
police force, international, 254-55
Polish girl in Portugal, story of, 12-13
politics, balance-of-power, 244-45, 247
Portugal, refugees and passengers in, 13-14
Poverty and *Poverty and Progress*, by Seebohm Rowntree, 40-41
Priestley, J. B., 34-36, 38, 73-74, 113
   Out of the People, 36
prisoners, German, treatment by English, 46
production, greater, need for, 253
psychology, need for use in defeat of the Axis, 219-20

Quislings, 205, 241

racial characteristics, 227
radio, German, on England, 45
   London speaking, 69-77
Ramsay, Captain and M. P., case and arrest, 116-17
Rashid Ali Beg Galiani, 149
reactionaries, 238
Red Star, Moscow, 148

INDEX

refugees in Portugal, 13-14
Reich, Das, 196
relief work, post-war, 240
resources, Axis and anti-Axis, 209-10
  mobilization for victory, 210-12
retribution for war crimes, 241-43
revolutions, causes of, 257
Reynaud, Paul, 207
Reynolds, Quentin, 76
Ribbentrop, Joachim von, 204
Roosevelt, Franklin Delano, 24, 141, 175, 211, 235
  airplane production schedule, 216
  Atlantic Charter, 229-31
  man of words and action, 82
  on pre-Hitler world, 229
  on the war, 179-80
Rowntree, Seebohm, *Poverty* and *Poverty and Progress,* 40-41
Rudenskys, 150-51
Rumania, 146, 147, 158
Russia. *See* Union of Soviet Socialist Republics
Russians, White, 13

Saracoglu, Foreign Minister, 146
scientists working against Hitler, 214
Serbia, 166
shelter, Anderson's, 30-31
Simon, Viscount, 96, 107
Simovitch, General, 147
Sinclair, Sir Archibald, 84, 106, 213
Slav Congress, 165
Slav regional federation, proposed, 243
Slavs, 165-66
Slovakia, 146
Socialism, international, 164
songs, war, in England, 55
Soviet Russia. *See* Union of Soviet Socialist Republics
Spain, 106-07, 154, 219
  in war time, 14-15
Spitfires (airplanes), 53
Stalin, Josef, 161, 191
  distrust of people, 23
  policy, new, 162
  prime minister, 148

Stalin, Josef (Cont.)
  turn to nationalism, 163-64
  See also Union of Soviet Socialist Republics
Strachey, John, 21
strategy of victory, 189-220
Strauss, George Russell, 30, 77, 131
Sunday Times, London, 224
Sweden, 209
Syria, 147

Tagus River, 10
Tait, Mrs. (M. P.), 115-16
tariffs, 250-52
Third International (Comintern), 164
Tolstoi, Alexei, 165
treaties, peace, after the first world war, 233
Tribune, The, 96
Tukhachevsky, Marshal, 153, 154
Turkey, 146

Union of Soviet Socialist Republics, 139-70
  and Turkey, 146
  attack by Germany, 27-28, 139-60
  Communism, 160-66
  dictatorship, 166-67
  factories, modern, 124
  industrialization, 122
  land question, 150
  language, 163
  leaders, 112
  nationalism, 161-64
  policy, foreign, ideal, 155-57
  post-war, 168-70, 243; and England, 242
  powerlessness in international affairs, 167-70
  propaganda, government, 228
  purge of 1937 and the Moscow trials, and the war, 152-55; reasons for the purge, 164
  questions, pre-war, put to Hitler, 146
  Slav Congress, 165
  treaty with Yugoslavia, 147
  trend from Communism, 161

INDEX

United States, and England, 101, 135-36; collaboration, post-war, 246
  and post-war Europe, 242, 243-44
  and the war, 142
  "arsenal of democracy," 211
  attack by Japan, 173-75, 182-85
  conscription of resources, for victory, 210-12
  in world affairs, 173-86
  isolationists, 175
  issue for America, in the war, 173
  peril of Fascism, 180-82
  post-war, aid for Europe, 169-70; leadership, 185-86
  reconstruction, world, American part in, 248-50
  relief work, post-war, 240
  role in peace, 247, 248
  tariff, 250-52
  war America's from the beginning, 174

Vansittart, Lord, and *Black Record*, 224-26
Vayo, Juan del, 29-30
Versailles Treaty, 226, 230, 232, 233, 250
  errors in, 234
victory, strategy of, 189-220

war, motorized and mechanized, 122
war, world, first, German defeat, 202-04
  peace treaties, 233
  responsibility for, 226
war, world, second, not inevitable, 176
  origin, 179
  reconstruction, post-war, 248-50
  responsibility for, 226-27
war, world, third, 238, 248, 259
Wardlaw-Milne, Sir John, 88
wars, causes of, 237-39, 244, 257
  prevention, 239
"wave of the future," 175
Wedgwood, Colonel Josiah, 131
Weller, George, 14
Welles, Sumner, 250
Wells, H. G., 74, 76
White Russians, 13
Wilder, Thornton, 76
Wilkinson, Ellen, 90
Wilson, Woodrow, 233
Winant, John G., 73
Winston, Captain, 5, 9, 10
Wood, Sir Kingsley, 95, 98
Woolton, Lord, 105, 106
world planning board, 253-54

York, England, 39-40
Yugoslavia, 147-49, 256
  treaty with Soviet Russia, 147

COLONIAL BOOK SERVICE
23 EAST 4th STREET
NEW YORK CITY 3, N. Y.
We Hunt Out-of-Print Books